Infection
Control

Infection Control

A *Community Perspective*

Edited by

Margaret A Worsley

Kate A Ward

Sue Privett

Lewis Parker

Janet M Roberts

Infection Control Nurses Association of the British Isles
First published by ICNA 1994
Copyright © ICNA, 1994.

ISBN 0 9515620 3 7

British Library Cataloguing in Publication Data.
A catalogue record of this book is available from
the British Library.

Designed by BRAZIL Design & Advertising

Contents

	Page
Introduction	I
Chapter 1 - Handwashing and Protective Clothing in Community Health Care Services	5
Chapter 2 - Health and Safety in General Practice	15
Chapter 3 - Infection Control for District Nursing	27
Chapter 4 - Infection Control in General Practice	33
Chapter 5 - Infection Control in Dentistry	43
Chapter 6 - Infection Control within Mental Healthcare Environments	49
Chapter 7 - Infection Control in Childcare Facilities	55
Chapter 8 - Infection Control and Day Surgery	61
Chapter 9 - Infection Control and the Ambulance Service	69
Chapter 10 - Public Health	79
Chapter 11 - Infection Control and Environmental Health	85
Chapter 12 - Guidance to Risk Management	93

We were delighted when The Infection Control Nurses Association sought our support in publishing this book. Our earlier collaboration in the preparation of *Infection Control, Guidelines for Nursing Care* was enjoyable and professionally satisfying. We viewed it as a valuable step in fulfilling our desire to form close ties with healthcare associations and this second book is evidence of our continuing commitment to that ideal.

Infection Control, A Community Perspective takes us into an environment where Johnson & Johnson has for a long time had an interest in developing advanced wound dressings and infection control products. By maintaining our close links with nursing professionals and listening to their views, we aim to support them with products which will make valuable contributions to the effective and economic treatment of patients.

We hope that you enjoy reading this book and that you find it a useful companion as a source of advice in your work. May I remind you that our company has a considerable resource available to you of further information in the form of literature, clinical reviews and videotape programmes. The Johnson & Johnson Medical Education Centre in Ascot would be very pleased to hear from you.

William C Strachan
Managing Director
Johnson & Johnson Medical Limited

These guidelines make a significant contribution to the recent changes in the delivery of healthcare; the emphasis has now moved away from the acute hospital environment into the community. The book promotes patient-centred care and ensures that quality and caring count as much as quantity and cost effectiveness.

The value of the guidelines is, as with the publication *'Infection Control, Guidelines for Nursing Care'*, that the team approach has been employed. The book is written in a clear and practical way, making it suitable for everyone with responsibilities for infection control, including managers, nurses, medical and ancillary staff. The Infection Control Nurses' Association is grateful to the authors and the editors. The latter have attempted to achieve consistency in presentation while retaining most of the author's individual style and overall approach to the subject of their chapter.

The publication of the book has been facilitated by individual members of Johnson & Johnson Medical, who willingly gave their support.

Janet M. Roberts.

Janet Roberts
Senior Infection Control Nurse
ICNA Chairman 1991-1994

Contributors

Authors

Miss Kate A. Ward,
Specialist Nurse Adviser Public Health,
Southern Derbyshire Health Authority.

Mrs Janet M. Roberts,
Senior Infection Control Nurse,
Wirral Hospital (NHS) Trust.

Mr David Morgan
Head of Scientific Affairs,
British Medical Association,
London.

Mrs Jean Lawrence,
Community Infection Control Nurse,
Leeds Community and Mental Health
Services (Teaching) Trust.

Dr J. K. Inman,
GP Committee,
British Medical Association,
London.

Mr Mike V. Martin,
Senior Lecturer/Consultant,
Oral Microbiology
Dept. Clinical Dental Services,
School of Dentistry,
University of Liverpool.

Ms Val Leggett,
Senior Nurse Specialist - Infection Control,
Norfolk Mental Health Care (NHS) Trust.

Mrs Sue Ross,
Infection Control Nurse,
Pinderfields Hospital (NHS) Trust.

Professor C. Wastell,
Professor of Surgery,
Chelsea & Westminster Hospital,
London

Mrs Debra Khan,
Community Infection Control Nurse,
Worcester and District Health Authority.

Dr Richard T. Mayon-White,
Consultant in Communicable Disease Control,
Oxfordshire Health Authority.

Mr M. Eastwood,
Director,
Northern School of Public Health,
School of Epidemiology,
Medical School, University of Manchester.

Mrs Jennifer East,
Infection Control Nurse,
Quality and Risk Management Specialists,
Infection Management Ltd.

Editors

Mrs Margaret A. Worsley,
Senior Nurse Manager Infection Control,
North Manchester Healthcare (NHS)
Trust, Manchester.

Miss Kate A. Ward,
Specialist Nurse Adviser Public Health,
Southern Derbyshire Health Authority.

Mrs Sue Privett,
Infection Control Nurse,
South Warwickshire General Hospital
(NHS) Trust.

Dr Lewis Parker
Consultant Microbiologist
(Retired)

Mrs Janet M. Roberts,
Senior Infection Control Nurse,
Wirral Hospital (NHS) Trust,
Chairman ICNA (1991-1994).

Foreword

O n behalf of the editorial team I am delighted to present to you a new publication from the Infection Control Nurses Association.

Infection Control: A Community Perspective is a follow-on to *Infection Control Nursing Guidelines* which was published in 1990.[1]

This new book moves away from the setting of the hospital and addresses the interface between the hospital and the community in the prevention and control of infection. A paradigm shift has occurred in the focus of care in the community;[2] therefore the time is right for the publication of this book.

Many issues that directly affect the outcome of patient care are addressed in this publication. We have invited authors who are experts in their particular field of infection control to present their own individual approach to the vast subject of infection prevention and control. These guidelines reflect the recent changes in the delivery of health care and public health.[3]

The advice offered is based on proven research[4,5] but also allows practitioners to use their own experience and intuition as described by Benner,[6] whilst maintaining safe practice.

This book is written in a practical way and will be useful for the health care worker in the community who is interested in the prevention and control of infection.

I would like to take the opportunity to thank the individual authors and my colleagues on the editorial team who have contributed to this important publication.

Mrs Margaret A. Worsley

REFERENCES
1. Worsley M A, Ward K, Parker L, Ayliffe G A J, Sedgwick J. Infection control guidelines for nursing care. London: ICNA, 1990.
2. Department of Health. Care in the Community. London: DOH, 1993.
3. Department of Health. HSG 93/56. Public Responsibilities of the NHS and the role of others. NHS/ME. London: DOH, 1993.
4. Department of Health. A vision for the future. London: DOH, 1993.
5. Kohner N. Clinical supervision in practice. Kings Fund Centre: Nursing Development Units, 1993.
6. Benner P. From novice to expert. California: Addison Wesley, 1984.

Miss Kate A. Ward

Infection Control -
A Community Perspective

Infection control practice has traditionally been seen as the prerogative of hospital staff and the problems of cross-infection as only affecting hospital patients. However, the ever shorter hospital stay coupled with minor surgery and other invasive clinical procedures being increasingly performed in, for example, general practices, has meant greater attention being paid to control of infection in the various community settings. The ongoing problem of communicable diseases, more often seen in the community than in the hospital setting, continues to present the threat of outbreaks involving large sections of the population. Some infections may have been judged to no longer present a problem to society but, as can be seen from the recent upsurge in tuberculosis, some infections will suddenly increase and once again require examination of methods of surveillance, prevention and control. Factors which make the population more vulnerable to infection continue to affect certain sections of the community, and services such as water and sewage need to be maintained to the highest standard.

Infection control has always been an important part of the public health function. During the 14th, 15th and 16th centuries the State attempted to control certain infections by quarantine registration and penalties.[1] For example, Edward II attempted to control leprosy in the city of London in 1346 by searching out lepers and banishing them. In 1529 Henry VII consulted the Royal College of Physicians for advice on the measures that would need to be taken to control the spread of plague. As a result, a system of registration of cases of plague and the Bills of Mortality were implemented.

In the 19th century an outbreak of cholera combined with a bad harvest, rising prices and unemployment created such alarm that the Government took the almost unprecedented step of ordering a public enquiry. This enquiry was carried out by three doctors under the direction of Edwin Chadwick, a civil servant. The devastating report in 1838 identified the extent of preventable disease and of the dreadful conditions under which people lived in the heart of London. Chadwick emphasised the crucial link between dirt, due to insanitary conditions and overcrowding, and disease. The report was followed by another investigation by Chadwick of 'the sanitary condition of the labouring poor'. The results of this investigation were published in 1842 in what is considered to be one of the most important documents on the life and conditions of Victorian England. Chadwick developed the theme that health depended on sanitation, and sanitation was largely a matter of engineering. He stressed both the economic cost of ill-health and the social cost in terms of its effect on morals and habits.

The Public Health Act, passed in 1848, established a General Board of Health for five years. Local boards of health were permitted to appoint a medical officer of health (MOH). Following the 1872 Act the new local sanitary authorities were also required to appoint MOsH. There were two main duties of the MOH. The first was sanitary inspection and improvement, and the second disease control. This control emphasised the need for primary isolation and the tracing of the source of infection in epidemics.

It was to be over a hundred years before The Public Health Act would be reviewed again. During the intervening years major changes occurred in the way in which infectious diseases, and infection in general, have been prevented and controlled. A protégé of Edwin Chadwick, Dr John Snow, was one of the first to demonstrate that disease did not arise from filth nor from miasmas (poisonous emanations from the earth). Whilst mapping the location of cholera cases in London during an epidemic in 1854, Snow noticed that there was a concentration of cases around a public water pump in Broad Street, Soho. The epidemic came to a fairly rapid end after he removed the handle of the pump. Following further investigations, from which he was able to demonstrate that the cleaner waters of the upper Thames were associated with a lower incidence of cholera, he concluded that diseases that are communicated from person to person were caused by some material which passed from the sick to the healthy. This material also had the ability to increase in the system of the person it attacked. It took a number of years for this and similar views to be accepted by the establishment and to be acted upon. It was a further 30 years before the causative organism, the cholera vibrio was discovered.

During the 1920s a general practitioner in Wensleydale, Dr William Pickles, identified the incubation periods of viral hepatitis (hepatitis A) and chickenpox simply by observing his patients. This information enabled more accurate quarantine and isolation times to be established for the control of these diseases.

The striking reduction in the death rate due to infectious disease, particularly in infants and children, has had a major impact on the overall pattern of mortality. There has been an enormous increase in the proportion of those who will live to be in their seventies. However, as previously mentioned, communicable diseases do continue to pose serious problems in vulnerable populations. Two such populations featured in outbreaks of infection in the mid 1980s which were to have a significant influence on the control of infection in hospitals and the community. The first outbreak of infection in 1984 occurred at the Stanley Royd Hospital when salmonella food poisoning, caused by poor kitchen hygiene, resulted in 19 deaths. The outbreak, in 1985, of Legionnaires' Disease at Stafford General Hospital was in effect a community outbreak as 101 outpatients were considered to be affected. Twenty-eight people died (22 definite cases and 6 possible). The two public inquiries which resulted from these outbreaks took place in 1986.[2,3] Both reports expressed anxiety about the availability and expertise in public health and communicable disease control.

In response the Government asked for a "broad and fundamental examination of the role of public health doctors" and for consideration to be given to the "future development of the public health function including the control of communicable diseases....". A committee under the chairmanship of the then Chief Medical Officer,

Sir Donald Acheson, reported in 1988. 'Public Health in England', or the Acheson Report as it is more widely known, provided a comprehensive review of the public health function and clearly defined the roles of the people and bodies involved in the control of communicable disease.[4] The major recommendation was that the Medical Officer of Environmental Health be replaced by a Consultant in Communicable Disease Control (CCDC). The CCDC would be responsible for linking the work of the microbiologists and control of infection teams within hospitals with cases of infection occurring in the community and be a source of public information on issues relating to the control of communicable disease and infection. More recently nurses have been appointed to work with the CsCDC in a similar way to the infection control teams in hospital and community trusts.

With the formation of trusts within the National Health Service there may be a temptation for health care workers at all levels to believe that any adverse effects that may occur as a result of poor infection control practice is only of consequence to their own area of work. This of course is far from the truth. For example, shorter lengths of stay mean that wound infections, in particular, are usually being dealt with by primary health care teams and patients with MRSA acquired in hospital wards are being dealt with by nursing and residential home staff. Equally, increasingly complex treatments being performed within the community settings mean that patients face the risk of acquiring infections from procedures performed by, for example, general practitioners, dentists, and chiropodists.

It is important that the general population is reassured that the care and treatments they receive are delivered in a safe manner. All health care staff working in either the primary or secondary care setting must receive adequate training and have available up-to-date research-based information to enable them to provide a high standard of infection control practice and to understand that infection control is everybody's business.

REFERENCES

1. Davies L G. The scope of public health. In : Davies L G, ed. Modern public health for medical students. 2nd ed., London: Edward Arnold, 1963.
2. Department of Health and Social Security, The Report of the Committee of Inquiry into an Outbreak of Food Poisoning at Stanley Royd Hospital, 1986, London: HMSO, 1986.
3. Department of Health and Social Security. Badenoch Sir J, First Report of the Committee of Inquiry into the Outbreak of Legionnaires' Disease in Stafford in April 1985. London: HMSO, 1986.
4. Department of Health and Social Security. Public Health in England, The Report of the Committee of Inquiry into the Future Development of the Public Health Function. London: HMSO, 1986.

Mrs Janet M. Roberts

Chapter 1

Handwashing and Protective Clothing in Community Health Care Services

Handwashing

'Now wash your hands' is a familiar slogan probably known to most of the British public, but despite the knowledge that washing hands helps prevent the spread of infection, compliance with the procedure is extremely low both in healthcare workers[1] and members of the public.

The reorganisation of the National Health Service and the Care in the Community Act have led to early discharge of patients from acute hospitals, exposing primary health care staff and patients to micro-organisms not previously encountered in healthcare facilities outside acute hospitals.

The role of the hands in the transmission of infection was convincingly demonstrated before the pathogenic role of micro-organisms was established. In 1847 Ignaz P. Semmelweis noted that 11.5% of the 4,010 women admitted to one clinic at the Vienna Maternity Hospital died of puerperal fever; whilst in another clinic, where all deliveries were carried out by midwives, the mortality rate was only 2.7%. Semmelweis concluded that puerperal fever in the first clinic was produced by contact with the contaminated hands of doctors and medical students from the post-mortem rooms. He demonstrated the truth of this conclusion by introducing handwashing with a chlorinated lime solution before internal examination. The result was a dramatic reduction in puerperal mortality to about 1%.[2] It is true today, as it was over a hundred years ago, that the simple action of handwashing remains the cornerstone of infection prevention. More recently handwashing has been demonstrated as being the most important method for preventing the spread of disease via the hands of children and personnel working in day care centres. Handwashing after toilet use and nappy changing has been shown to limit the spread of enteric infections[3] and centres with formal handwashing procedures had a lower incidence of contamination of both hands and nursery items.[4] Price[5] was the first to divide the bacteria on normal skin into 'transient' and 'resident', a classification still relevant today, especially for education, training and research purposes. Transient bacteria are relatively scarce on clean skin, since these are acquired from extraneous sources, literally 'by hand'. There is no limit to the varieties, both pathogenic and non-pathogenic; that may be 'in transit' on the skin at any one time. They lie free on the skin or are loosely attached by fats along with dirt. Resident bacteria, the normal flora, are a relatively stable population, both in size and composition; any increase is due mainly to the natural multiplication of the microflora already present.

The term Hygienic Hand Disinfection (HHD) originated in Europe and describes more accurately what good handwashing really is. The aim of HHD[6] is to ensure that no pathogenic (transient) or potentially pathogenic (resident) micro-organisms are transferred via the hands.

In community healthcare facilities and situations where the likelihood of cross

infection occurs, e.g. in day care centres, long term facilities, nursing homes and when caring for patients/clients in their own homes by community based healthcare staff, the objectives of HHD are:
- to remove all pathogenic micro-organisms (transients) from the hands, before and after every physical contact and after handling articles which are likely to be contaminated;
- to prevent micro-organisms that may have contaminated the hands being transferred to other people or articles, thereby causing infection;
- to reduce the number of potentially pathogenic organisms on the hands of staff/carers, immediately before elective aseptic procedures;
- to prevent micro-organisms from the patient/client becoming established on the hands of staff.

HHD can be achieved in two ways:
- by washing with soap under running water;
- if the hands are physically clean by rubbing with a prepared 70% isopropyl alcohol solution.

Techniques for attaining thorough hand disinfection are shown in Table 1, together with procedures and pitfalls when using the methods and the indications for HHD and the wearing of gloves.[7]

The number of resident skin bacteria can be reduced mechanically by energetic frictional handwashing, however it is the transient skin micro-organisms that are readily transferred from person to person and are a health hazard; washing with soap and water alone, using the recommended technique, will remove 90% of these.[8]

The principles of HHD can be applied to all situations likely to be encountered in the community. The quality of handwashing will still largely depend on the educational methods employed and the dissemination of the available information. Using experience from the hospital setting it was shown in a recent study[1] that, despite a comprehensive educational and promotional campaign, handwashing frequencies soon returned to pre-campaign levels. It was concluded that a lack of motivation is the most important cause of low compliance rather than a lack of knowledge. Childhood experiences influence handwashing behaviour; therefore, educational programmes aimed at teaching these principles in day care centres, nurseries and primary schools should be encouraged. Patient education regarding the importance of handwashing in preventing adverse outcomes may encourage compliance by health care workers. It is unlikely that any single strategy will work in increasing these behaviours, it needs a concerted effort at all times by healthcare workers to ensure more compliance with this simple procedure.

Table 1

Techniques

Handwashing with soap alone ....

1 Wet hands under running water.
2 Dispense one dose of soap into a cupped hand.
3 Handwash for 15-30 seconds vigorously and thoroughly, without adding more water.
4 Rinse hands thoroughly under running water.
5 Dry hands with a paper towel.

Pitfalls
· Using too much soap.
· Adding more water whilst handwashing.
· Handwashing for longer than 1 minute.

Handrubbing with alcohol alone instead of handwashing with soap ....

1 Dispense 2-3 ml of alcohol into cupped hands.
2 Handrub to dryness (alcohol evaporates in about 25 seconds) vigorously and thoroughly, without adding more alcohol.

Pitfalls
· Using too much alcohol.
· Omitting to wash soiled hands with soap before rubbing with alcohol.
· Handwashing after an alcohol rub.

Handwashing with soap followed by handrubbing with alcohol ....

Techniques for attaining thorough handwashing with soap or handrubbing with alcohol

1 Rub palm to palm.
2 Rub right palm over back of left hand and vice versa.
3 Rub palm to palm, with two fingers interlaced.
4 Rub right palm over back of left hand, with fingers interlaced and vice versa.
5 Rub right finger tips into left palm and vice versa.
6 Clasp left thumb with right hand, rub rotationally and vice versa.
7 Rub left wrist with right hand and vice versa.

Please see over for Indications

Table 1 continued

Indications

	Soap	Alcohol	Gloves*
At the beginning and end of clinical duties	•		
When hands are visibly soiled	•		
Immediately after hands have been contaminated with blood, faeces, urine, or other biological fluids, or is anticipated			✔
Between every physical contact with patients, even if hands remain visibly clean		•	
Before elective aseptic procedures (e.g. minor procedures, insertion of lines, collection of specimens for microbiological investigation from sites which are normally sterile)	•	•	
Before emergency aseptic procedures			✔
Before serving food	•		
Before and after going to the toilet	•		

* Gloves are not a substitute for hygienic hand disinfection
  and are not to be considered as an absolute barrier,
  whether in protecting the patient or staff.

Protective Clothing

The use of protective clothing is only one aspect of an infection control programme and should not be treated in isolation from other aspects of patient/client care. Protective clothing may be worn for a variety of reasons but usually for one or more of those listed:

- to prevent the user's clothing or uniform becoming contaminated with pathogenic micro-organisms which may be subsequently transferred to other patients/clients in their care;
- to prevent the user's clothing or uniform becoming soiled, wet or stained during the course of their duties;
- to prevent the direct transfer or dissemination of potentially pathogenic micro-organisms from the user to the patient/client;
- to protect the user from acquiring an infection from the patient/client[9]

The regulations of the Health and Safety Commission require that employers ensure that personal protective clothing is available to all employees,[10] and that the protective clothing is in fact worn. All healthcare workers should have training, information and instruction on the use and purpose of protective clothing. Advice should be sought from persons with the knowledge and expertise on the use of protective clothing and its care or disposal, particularly in special situations or unusual circumstances where a risk analysis needs to be made.[11] However in situations where staff wear personal clothing it must be practical, clean and washable. Sleeve length should not restrict HHD techniques and a change of clothing should be available for staff if contaminated with body fluids or excreta.[12]

There is far more awareness amongst clinical staff and the public about the risks associated with infectious agents and the use of protective clothing has increased accordingly. However, the routes of transmission of these micro-organisms are much less well known and unfortunately this has led to the inappropriate choice and usage of such clothing.[13] This could result in inadequate protection for patients and healthcare workers and may have considerable financial implications.

Aprons/Gowns

Research shows that cotton is not an effective barrier to bacteria and confers no protection to the wearer against moisture and wetness.[14] Therefore there is no rationale for wearing gowns even for minor surgical procedures in clinics or surgeries. Cotton tabards are frequently worn to protect personal clothing of staff when caring for babies and young children in nurseries or other day care and long term facilities. They should be changed daily and laundered at 65°C for not less than 10 minutes, or 71°C for not less than three minutes, to achieve adequate disinfection.[15]

Plastic aprons are the most effective and practical barrier against contamination, being impermeable to both moisture and bacteria. Although aprons do not provide protection to the shoulder area of the wearer the levels of micro-organisms found on this area are insignificant.[16] Plastic disposable aprons are most suitable, they are inexpensive and may be used on more than one occasion for the same patient or client providing they are stored dry between use.

The surface of both plastic aprons and plasticised cotton aprons may be adequately disinfected between use by wiping over with a solution of liquid detergent and hot water and drying, followed by wiping over with a 70% isopropyl alcohol impregnated wipe. This method is more suitable for the expensive aprons and tabards and is not recommended as routine for plastic aprons designed to be disposable as it is time consuming and the disinfectant wipes will cost more than the plastic apron itself.

Caps/Hats

The wearing of caps/hats as protective clothing is only recommended in food preparation areas. It is recognised that hair can carry *Staphylococcus aureus*[17] although this is usually secondary to nasal carriage or settlement from the air, and should these bacteria contaminate food prior to its consumption they may cause food poisoning. Thorough handwashing by the staff preparing the food and measures to prevent cross-contamination in the kitchens are far more important. Cross infection associated with hair carriage is most likely to occur when there is a scalp infection present. In such an instance the member of staff should be excluded from work until the infection is treated.[18]

Gloves

It is essential to bear in mind that the wearing of gloves does not preclude the need for handwashing because of the variable integrity of the gloves.[19] Some gloves have minute holes which allow bacteria to pass through. Gloves do not give protection against needlestick or sharps penetration. The heat processes used in the manufacture of disposable gloves destroy micro-organisms and providing that the gloves are stored in a manner likely to avoid contamination, either by air or contact, they are suitable for those occasions when the use of sterile gloves would merely be a waste of money. Sterile gloves are approximately twice the price of the same quality clean gloves. In most instances sterile gloves do not confer any advantage over clean gloves except during sterile surgical procedures, e.g. minor operations, or manipulation of sterile equipment, such as changing of lines in intravenous therapy. In response to increasing concern over the risk of HIV, hepatitis B and other infections among healthcare workers, it has been recommended that gloves are worn for all procedures in which it is anticipated that there will be contact with blood and body fluids and when handling infectious materials.[20, 21] This emphasis on gloving has led to healthcare workers washing gloves instead of changing them, partly due to the economic advantage and partly due to the shortage of disposable gloves. This is especially true in developing countries where gloves are not readily available and costs are prohibitive. It is recognised that the washing and re-use of gloves will occur in some situations, although medical gloves are not designed to be washed or disinfected for reuse. Although it is possible to reduce contamination on gloves by washing it is not intended that healthcare workers use recycled gloves for procedures where proper gloving is critical for patient rather than staff safety.Rubber household gloves which are designed to be used many times should be worn for cleaning purposes and for protection from chemicals known to cause skin reactions. They should be washed, rinsed and thoroughly dried prior to removal and storage. The hands are the most likely means of transmission of infection and this risk will be minimised by thorough handwashing and the judicious use of gloves.

Masks
Research does not support the wearing of masks in many circumstances[22] and in hospitals today masks are rarely worn outside the operating theatres; even then their usefulness is questionable. The rationale for wearing a mask is either to protect the patient/client from the staff or vice versa. It is most unusual for organisms which cause wound infections to be disseminated in droplets from the mouth and nose. It is more likely to be spread by hand contact through staff handling the mask in use or after use. The wearing of masks by staff suffering from colds or sore throats is inappropriate; such staff should not be on duty.

Eye Protection
Where the transmission of blood-borne viruses is possible through blood splashing onto mucous membranes and/or conjunctiva, eye protection should be worn. Protection is recommended for use in orthopaedic surgery when flying bone fragments are also a possibility; in gynaecological and obstetrical procedures; in dentistry and in endoscopy units and for protection against splashes with chemicals.[23, 24, 25, 26]

The types of eye protection available are as follow and must conform with British standards:
- safety spectacles with extended arms which can also be made up with prescription lenses for those staff who normally wear spectacles;
- visors, some of which are incorporated with a disposable face mask;
- goggles.

It is important to ensure that non-disposable eye protection is disinfected after use. Washing in a solution of liquid detergent and hot water and drying thoroughly is adequate disinfection process.

Overshoes

There is no evidence to suggest that using disposable overshoes is of any benefit to patients in the transmission of infection.[27] On the contrary, the hazards associated with them include dispersal of the bacteria due to the bellows action when walking and, more importantly, the transfer of bacteria from the floor to the hands when applying and removing the overshoes.[28]

As part of protective clothing there is no justification for wearing overshoes and therefore they are not recommended.

Conclusion

In situations where there is uncertainty regarding the correct choice of protective clothing or whether protection is required, infection control nurses working either in the local hospital or in the community are available to give expert advice and guidance. This will avoid the unnecessary wastage of materials and finance and staff will be secure in the knowledge that safe practices are being employed for the benefit of themselves and their patients.

REFERENCES
1. Buckles A, Williams E. A lack of motivation. The Journal of Infection Control Nursing. Nursing Times 1988; 84 (22): 60-64.
2. Ackerknecht E H. A short history of medicine. Baltimore: Johns Hopkins University Press, 1982.
3. Black R B, Dykes A C, Anderson K E, et al. Handwashing to prevent diarrhoea in day care centers. Am J Epidemiol 1981; 113: 4.
4. Holoday B, Pantell R H, Lewis C C, Gillis C L. Patterns of faecal coliform contamination in day care centres. Public Health Nursing 1990; 7(4): 224-7.
5. Price P B. The bacteriology of normal skin. J Infect Dis 1938; 63: 301-18.
6. Ayliffe G A J, Babb J R, Quoraishi A H. A test for 'hygienic' hand disinfection. J Clin Pathol 1978; 31: 923-928.
7. Bartzokas C A, Roberts J M. Hygienic hand disinfection. Indications and Procedures. One of a series of educational publications, produced for the Wirral Hospitals, by the Infection Control Service 1992.
8. Ayliffe G A J, Collins B J, Taylor L J. Hospital acquired infections: principles and prevention 2nd ed. London: Wright, 1990.
9. Ayton M, Babb J R, Mackintosh C A, Maloney M. Report of an Infection Control Nurses' Association Working Party on Protective Clothing, 1984.
10. Health and Safety Executive. Personal protective equipment at work regulations. Guidance on Regulations, Leeds: HSE 1992.
11. Department of Health. Risk Management in the NHS. London: NHS Management Executive, 1993.
12. Walker A, Donaldson B. Infection control. dressing for protection. Nursing Times 1993; 89(2): 60-2.
13. Loomes S, Vincent J, Wilson J, Worthington D. The wearing of protective clothing report. Trent Group: Infection Control Nurses' Association, 1993.
14. Wilson J L. The price of protection. Nursing Times, 1990; 86(26): 67-8.
15. Department of Health and Social Services. Health Circular. Hospital laundry arrangements for used and infected linen. 1987, December, HC(87):30.
16. Babb J R, Davies J G, Ayliffe G A J. Contamination of protective clothing and nurses' uniforms in an isolation ward. J Hosp Infect 1983: 4: 149-57.
17. Black W A, Bannerman C M, Black D A. Carriage of potentially pathogenic bacteria in the hair. Br J Surg 1974; 61: 735-8.
18. Dineen P, Drusin L. Epidemics of postoperative wound infections associated with hair carriers. Lancet 1973; ii: 1157-9.
19. Yangco B G, Yangco N F. What is leaky can be risky: a study of the integrity of hospital gloves. Infect Control Hosp Epidemiol. 1989; 10(12): 553-6.
20. Royal College of Nursing. Nursing guidelines on the management of patients in the hospital and community suffering from AIDS. AIDS Working Party, 2nd report. London: RCN, 1986.
21. Update: Universal precautions for prevention of transmission of Human Immunodeficiency Virus, Hepatitis B virus, and other blood-borne pathogens in healthcare settings. MMWR/1988; 37(24): 377-82, 387-8.
22. Ayliffe G A J, Lowbury E J, Geddes A M, Williams J D. Control of hospital infection; a practical handbook. 3rd ed. London: Chapman and Hall, 1992.
23. Acheson D. Guidance for clinical health care workers, protection against infection with HIV and hepatitis viruses, Recommendations of the Expert Advisory Group on AIDS, Department of Health. London: HMSO, 1992.

24. Royal College of Obstetricians and Gynaecologists, HIV Infection in maternity care and gynaecology, Revised report of a subcommittee on problems associated with AIDS in relation to obstetrics and gynaecology. London: RCOG, 1990.
25. Duthie G S, Johnson S R, Packer G J, Mackie I G. Eye protection, HIV and orthopaedic surgery (letter). Lancet 1988; i: 481-2.
26. Glenwright H D, Martin M V. Occasional Paper number 2, Infection control in dentistry; A practitioners guide. London: British Dental Association, 1993.
27. Jones M, Jakeways M. Theatre Nursing Over-estimating Overshoes. Nursing Times, 1988; 84(41): 66-71.
28. Carter R. Ritual and Risk. Journal of Infection Control Nursing. Nursing Times 1990: 86(13): 63-4.

Mr David Morgan

Chapter 2

Health and Safety in General Practice

Introduction

During the past forty years of the National Health Service general medical practice has greatly expanded and consolidated its role in providing first-line health care services to the UK population. The number of general practitioners (GPs) has increased from about 18,000 in 1949 to well over 32,000 in 1994, supported by a further 2,700 GP trainees and assistants, and approximately 16,000 practice nurses. As an employer the GP assumes a number of important responsibilities affecting the general practice environment and the health and safety of employees, and anyone else who enters the premises.

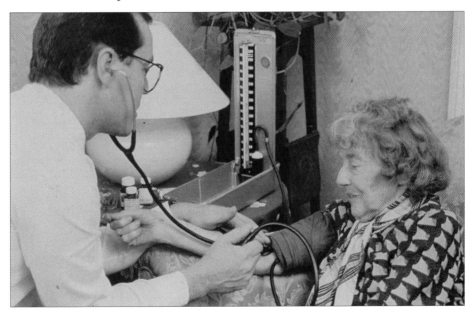

Elderly or infirm patients may be at particular risk of injury and need safe access to surgeries

The GP has a contract to supply services to patients on a list who are registered by the Family Health Services Authority (FHSA). It is the GP's responsibility to provide the premises, time, equipment and systems to do an appropriate job, and within the broad guidelines of the contract there is considerable flexibility about how and where this service is provided. The contract between the general practitioner and the FHSA contains agreements about hours of work, access by patients, and standards of premises. The FHSA has the responsibility of planning, developing and managing services provided by general medical practitioners, general dental practitioners, retail pharmacists and opticians. The role of the FHSAs includes supporting continuing education for the staff in practices, encouraging medical audit as well as traditional tasks such as approving surgery locations, hours of availability, inspecting premises, and checking standards of equipment, e.g. for minor surgery.

General Practice Surgeries

Surgery premises are included in the 'health services' grouping and are subject to Health and Safety at Work etc. Act 1974, and to inspection by officials of the Health and Safety Executive (HSE). Officials may visit GP surgeries from time to time to ensure that the general practitioners are maintaining a healthy and safe working environment. The main aim of the Health and Safety at Work etc Act. 1974 is to ensure that both the employers and the employees do all that is reasonably practicable to ensure a safe working environment. The general practitioner must ensure that particular hazards or risk of injury have been assessed and action taken to reduce the risk of injury as far as possible.

The regulations on notifying accidents are relevant to general practitioners; they impose a statutory obligation on all employers to keep a record of any accidents occurring on their premises. The general practitioner is liable as the 'controller of the premises' to notify the Health and Safety Executive of certain serious accidents to their own staff and to anyone else who may be on the premises, such as patients, workmen, or health authority staff. Notifiable accidents which must be reported to the Health and Safety Executive are fatal accidents, or those causing major injury, for instance fracture of the skull or pelvis. There is also a duty to report if a person has been incapacitated for more than three consecutive days as a result of an accident at work, and if an employee has suffered from a reportable condition and then dies from it within one year. However, general practice staff should report all accidents, such as sharps injuries, to their supervisor or general practitioner. Such accidents must be recorded in the accident book and any necessary treatment undertaken.

Although the Health and Safety at Work etc Act. 1974 is mostly concerned with the safety of employees, the employer also has a duty to ensure the safety of anyone who enters the surgery or health centre and this will include company representatives, tradesmen and health authority staff. The Act requires the practice to be organised so as to ensure that all users of the premises are safe from risks of personal injury, as the Occupiers Liability Act 1957 lays down a 'common duty of care' owed to all persons using the premises.

Physical Hazards

There are many physical and electrical hazards in a general practice environment such as word processing equipment, photocopying machines, electrical switches; and specialised equipment such as autoclaves; and hazardous chemicals. It is advisable for all general practitioners to prepare a written safety policy for their employees, although this is mandatory only for those with five or more staff. Such a policy even if it is brief and simple should be as comprehensive as possible so that both the GP and the safety inspector can ensure that the procedures are adequate. In the expansion of computer technology in the workplace, general practice has been no exception. The Display Screen Equipment Regulations 1992 which came into force on 1 January 1993, place specific duties on employers with regard to visual display unit (VDU) users. Staff who use VDU equipment need to avoid eye strain, have comfortable seating and be able to adjust the brightness and contrast of the screen image. Staff will require to take short but frequent breaks away from the VDU equipment. Employees who are covered by the regulations can ask for an eye test.

The Manual Handling Operations Regulations 1992 require that employers should identify all manual handling operations undertaken by employees, and provide training and instruction to enable them to safely undertake any necessary handling. The use of mechanical aids, e.g. a sack truck, should be considered when reasonably practicable to improve safety and also productivity.

Implementation of the Provision and Use of Work Equipment Regulations 1992 applies to all sectors of work activity where any machine, apparatus, tool or installation used at work is involved. The employer must ensure that work equipment is suitable, without risks to health or safety, and is adequately maintained. Control systems must be safe and breakdown or damage must not result in danger.

Control of Substances Hazardous to Health (COSHH Regulations)

The meaning of a substance hazardous to health is set out in the Control of Substances Hazardous to Health (COSHH) Regulations 1988. It covers any form of substance (solid, liquid, gas, fume, vapour) and any category (including micro-organisms and allergens) that are capable of damaging health through being absorbed, injected, inhaled or ingested; or generated out of, or in connection with, any work activity undertaken in the surgery.

The COSHH regulations give a clear responsibility to general practitioners to ensure that the risks to health of employees are controlled adequately. Fundamental to this is the need to undertake an assessment of the risks to health created by any work activity. Consequently, this will enable the GPs to make appropriate decisions about measures necessary to control hazardous substances or activities as a result of the work in general practice. In addition it requires the GP to:

- assess the risk to health arising from work and take what precautions are needed;
- introduce appropriate measures to prevent or control risk;
- ensure that control measures are used, equipment is properly maintained and procedures observed;
- monitor where necessary, the exposure of employees and carry out an appropriate form of health surveillance;
- inform, instruct and train employees about the risks and precautions to be taken.

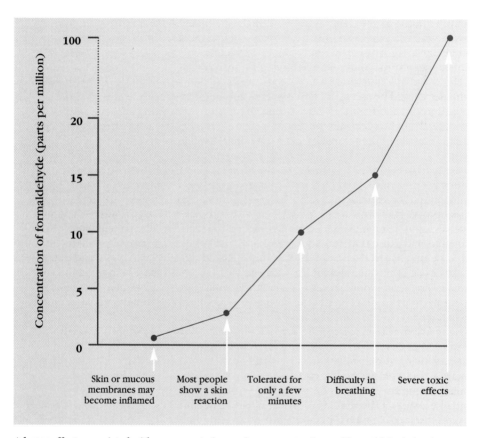

Adverse effects associated with exposure to increasing concentrations of formaldehyde in air

The COSHH assessment will take account of hazard evaluation, the degree of toxicity or harmful effect which can be ascribed to a particular substance used in the practice. Great care should be taken with substances of unknown toxicity which may be used, for example, as disinfectants.

The assessment of exposure will take into account factors which relate both to the substance and to the activity being carried out, for example whether dust or aerosols are produced, the potential for exposure during use and the likely route, i.e. dermal or by inhalation or inoculation. A risk assessment for a particular procedure should combine the information on the hazard and the potential exposure considered above. The end result should be a ranking of the exposure potential as high, medium or low and this should take account of the necessary containment required. For example the use of gluteraldehyde as a disinfectant in general practice should only be allowed when such assessments have been undertaken, and the risk of injury to staff has been reduced by proper venting and containment of the liquid. Alternative disinfectants or procedures should always be considered.

The use of all chemical substances including cleaning materials and prescribed medicines should be assessed. Staff dispensing or handling medicines may be exposed to risk and hence an assessment is required. Some drugs such as antibiotics or chemicals such as formalin or glutaraldehyde carry a risk of occupational asthma and those handling them must be offered regular respiratory review.

Biological Hazards
Under the terms of COSHH regulation, hepatitis B is a microbiological hazard and general practitioners should ensure that they and their staff receive proper protection. All staff who are likely to be exposed to blood or body fluids including those at risk of being bitten or scratched by patients, those taking or handling specimens and those undertaking or assisting with surgical and dental procedures should be vaccinated. Needlestick injury and mucous membrane exposure to blood provide a risk of transmission of blood-borne viruses.[1, 2] Staff must be trained to avoid sharps injuries and blood exposures, and a procedure should be established for dealing with such events.[3, 4] Adequate staff protection and cleaning materials should be available to remove potential biohazards, such as vomit, faeces and blood spillages. There is increasing concern that Hepatitis C Virus (HCV) and HIV could be transmitted in general practice settings and, in the absence of vaccination or treatment being available, health care workers must ensure that they avoid infection by scrupulous attention to infection control procedures. Every general practice should provide an infection control policy for all staff to implement. Employees should be aware of the reasons for using effective decontamination measures, know the circumstances in which personal protective equipment and clothing are needed, and avoid resheathing of contaminated needles.

Clinical Waste
General practitioners and practice nurses are major producers of clinical waste, including contaminated sharps. To comply with the Health and Safety at Work etc. Act 1974, suitable containers should be available in the surgery to collect sharps and biological waste material.

When an injection is carried out at a patient's home a GP must ensure that the syringe, needle and any used ampoule is safely contained in a suitable sharps box and returned to the surgery for safe disposal. The normal domestic waste should be housed appropriately and special arrangements provided for clinical waste, hazardous items, sharps bins etc. Under the Environmental Protection Act 1990, a duty of care has now been placed on those dealing with controlled waste. The duty

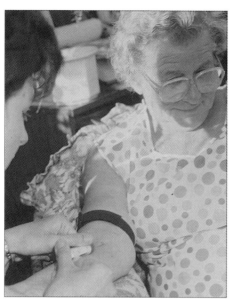

When administering an injection at a patient's home, GPs must ensure that the syringe is disposed of safely

requires those responsible for controlled waste to take all reasonable measures to:
- prevent it causing environmental pollution or harm to human health;
- ensure that it does not escape from their control (e.g. by packaging it securely);
- ensure that it is handled only by someone authorised to receive it (e.g. a registered waste carrier or disposal licence holder);
- to ensure that, when waste is transferred, a transfer note, sufficiently describing the waste, is handed to the recipient.

Risk of Infection

The lack of informative reviews on general practice decontamination has been commented on by researchers in the very few surveys that have looked at general practice infection control procedures.[5, 6] The literature contains few case reports of cross infection from instruments in doctors' surgeries; however, many cases probably go unrecognised.[7]

Although hepatitis B virus transmission predominantly occurs from patients to health care workers, a number of instances of transmission from health care workers to patients have been reported, and generally involves oral surgeons, dentists and surgeons who are chronic carriers of hepatitis e antigen (HBeAg). Other health care staff have also been implicated and anyone undertaking invasive procedures, such as minor surgery, could risk transmission. In the UK during the period 1985 to 1988, 3% of reported acute hepatitis B cases had a history of recent surgical or dental treatment and between 1975 and 1990 there were 12 hospital outbreaks; many cases may be subclinical however, and go unreported. The first case of possible transmission of HIV from a dentist to six patients has been reported[8] in the US, and clusters of patient-to-patient transmission of HIV and HCV are under investigation.[9, 10] Earlier, Skegg and Paul,[11] pointed out the paradox that campaigns to screen women for cervical neoplasia could actually propagate the disease by transmitting human papilloma virus, if specula were not properly decontaminated.

Worldwide there are now 64 cases of documented occupationally acquired HIV infections in health care staff, with a further 118 cases presumed.[12] Each year in the United States several thousand health care workers are infected with hepatitis B and, for many, this is the result of cross infection from their patients.[13] The failure to vaccinate all those at risk in the US has been acknowledged and many European countries are now considering how they can promote hepatitis B vaccination for all staff who are at risk of infection. Guidelines from the United Kingdom Department of Health make it mandatory for surgeons, doctors and their colleagues undertaking invasive procedures to show immunity to hepatitis B virus;[14] probably only about half of GPs have been immunised.[15] Hepatitis B virus is very infectious with a transmission risk as high as 30% following a deep needlestick injury, with transfer of patient blood. HIV is much less infectious with about a 1 in 300 (0.3%) risk. The risk for HCV has yet to be quantified but could be much higher; in the region of 1 in 30.

With HIV or HCV however, there is little likelihood of a vaccine being available for many years, if at all, and the risk of occupational infection and cross infection between patients will increase as the prevalence of infection builds up in the patient population, and as more invasive techniques are employed in general practice.

Compliance with Infection Control Recommendations

In the United Kingdom, one recent report[6] indicated that only 8% of practices had autoclaves and a second[5] found only 25%. A subsequent national postal survey of UK GPs, showed that nearly half of practices in the study had installed an autoclave, although some instruments were receiving inadequate decontamination.[16] A large study of general practitioners[17] found that, although many doctors had changed procedures and equipment because of HIV infection and were wearing gloves for venepuncture, 22.6% of GPs had incorrectly adopted resheathing of needles. The GPs were uncertain about the risks of infection associated with the needlestick injury, more than half had no policy for controlling infection, although nearly 78% would take patient blood for an HIV antibody test and 29% would allow their practice nurse to do so.

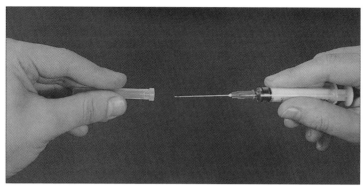

Up to 40% of all needlestick injuries involve resheathing or recapping the needle after use

a) The health care worker aims the needle towards the resheathing cap and

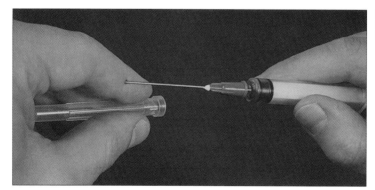

b) misses, jabbing the hand holding the cap

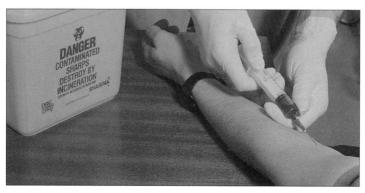

Venepuncture carries some risk of injury to health care staff including the accidental inoculation of blood and transmission of disease

The possibility that nurses are failing to adopt routine infection control procedures has been identified in the literature on nursing and HIV/AIDS. For example in a survey of Norwegian hospital workers, 63% reported daily exposure to potentially infectious situations, but only 23% said they used gloves for invasive procedures.[18] Similar findings were reported in a small study of practice nurses in England, where over half the nurses said they had suffered needlestick injury and a quarter reported accidents involving spilling or splashing of blood.[19]

In a further small study, over two-thirds of the nurses sampled were not using the recommended infection control procedures routinely; they reported not wearing gloves when handling open wounds and dressings, being careless with spillages of blood and body fluids and not adopting other precautions such as the wearing of goggles to protect their eyes.[20]

In 1989 the British Medical Association published a code of practice on the sterilisation of instruments and control of cross infection in response to the need for central guidelines in general practice and this has been widely distributed in the United Kingdom.[21] This publication sets standards for decontamination, provides a practical training manual for general practitioners and their staff, and if followed, provides assurance of a general practitioner's compliance with health and safety legislation. A key recommendation is the provision of an autoclave for sterilisation of instruments, rather than hot water systems or disinfectants, and an infection control policy.[21] A further code of practice provides guidelines for the safe use and disposal of sharps.[22]

Infection Control Policy

Typically, a general practice infection control policy would need to address the following issues:

- protective clothing, when to wear gloves, aprons etc. and how to dispose of, or clean, contaminated items;
- prohibition of eating, drinking, and smoking, except in designated areas;
- basic hygiene, hand washing and decontamination of surfaces;
- procedures for pre-cleaning, sterilising and disinfecting instruments;
- how to load and operate autoclaves, disinfectors and hot air ovens, including guidance on changing water, switching on machine, frequency of servicing;
- chemical disinfectants, appropriate chemicals for different purposes, advice on handling and storing disinfectants, use of extractors to remove fumes;
- disposal of clinical waste, what constitutes clinical waste, where to store waste prior to collection, arrangement with FHSA for delivery of yellow bags and sharps bins and collection of waste for incineration;
- procedure for accidents, especially needlestick injury, first-aid treatment, whom to notify, logging incidents in accident book.

Discussion

The Council of the European Communities has accepted a new code of practice which employers are required to put into place by 30 April 1994 (by 31 December 1995 for Portugal [Directive 90/679/EEC]). Under the new code, all EC employers will have to carry out a risk assessment of workers to identify those exposed to any virus or bacteria. Workers must be advised of infection risks and, in the case of hepatitis B, offered vaccination. The key to protection is education and training, and provision of resources.

Both initial and continuing training for GPs and their staff in infection control is important. Post Registration Education and Practice (PREP) has been designed as a way of setting standards for all nurses, midwives and health visitors to improve patient and client care. In order to remain on the register, nurses, midwives and health visitors specifically will need to comply with a number of requirements. Each practitioner will have to undertake a minimum of five days study leave in each three-year period leading to re-registration; study time must be spent in activities relevant to the practitioner's professional responsibilities and tailored to the individual needs.

At present there are no requirements for reaccreditation once a GP principal is on the minor surgery list. Such a position in respect of minor surgery is untenable today, particularly as a number of medical Royal Colleges move towards introducing systems of reaccreditation or recertification for their members.[23] The minor surgery regulations contain no requirement to perform any formal audit of minor surgery services within a practice, although it would be prudent to carry out routine audit, and the adoption of audit is one of the recommendations of the minor surgery guidelines.[24]

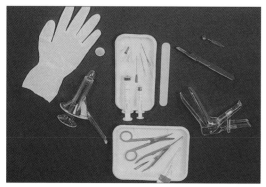

A wide range of single use (disposable) instruments is now available for use in general practice. After use the items must be disposed of safely and must not be reused. Single-use items are convenient for situations where other decontamination procedures cannot be carried out effectively, for instance during home visits and in the community or branch surgery.

National guidelines for sterilisation of instruments and control of cross infection[21] and for the safe use and disposal of sharps[22] are therefore essential for training medical students and nurses, and will help general practitioners to establish practice policies. The real risk of transmission of HIV and other blood-borne viruses between patients or from patients to staff or vice versa remains small, but any transmission that does occur will have important consequences for those involved. It will be essential for all general practitioners to ensure that staff who are at risk of infection become well trained in infection control practices and are motivated to adopt safe clinical procedures.

Infection control should be part of assuring a quality service, and guidelines on good practice in infection control should be the standards used in the audit process to ensure continuous quality improvement. The British Standard BS7750 specifies the elements of a general environmental management system which is intended to apply to all types and sizes of organisations and lends itself to all aspects of the health care sector, including general practice. It is only by reviewing practice in infection control that the risk of infection can be reduced and quality of care increased. Monitoring the effectiveness of infection control programmes is a way of measuring outcomes and therefore reflects the quality of care given to patients.[25]

REFERENCES
1. Morgan D R. HIV and needlestick injuries. Lancet 1990; 335: 1280.
2. Morgan D R. Infection control and risk assessment: a review, a pilot study and recommendations, Int J Risk and Safety Med 1992; 3:241-52.
3. Morgan D R. Needlestick Injuries: How can we teach people better about risk assessment? J Hosp Infect 1988; 12:301-309.
4. Morgan D R. Preventing needlestick injuries. Br Med J 1991; 302: 1147.
5. Hoffman P N, Cooke E M, Larkin D P, et al. Control of infection in general practice: a survey and recommendations. Br Med J 1988; 297: 34-6.
6. Farrow S C, Kaul S, Littlepage B C. Disinfection methods in general practice and health authority clinics: a telephone survey. J Roy Coll Gen Pract 1988; 38:447-9.
7. Drummond D C, Skidmore A G. Sterilisation and disinfection in the physicians' office. Can Med Assoc J 1991; 145: 937-43.
8. From the Centers for Disease Control and Prevention. Update: investigations of persons treated by HIV-infected health care workers. United States: JAMA 1993; 269:2622-3.
9. Chant K, Lowe D, Rubin G, et al. Patient-to-patient transmission of HIV in private surgical consulting rooms. Lancet 1993; 342: 1548-9.
10. BMJ News. Australians investigate hepatitis C cases. Br Med J 1994; 308: 1256-7.
11. Skegg D C, Paul C. Viruses, specula and cervical cancer. Lancet 1986; i: 797.
12. Heptonstall J, Gill O N, Porter K, Black M B, Gilbart V L. Health care workers and HIV: surveillance of occupationally acquired infection in the United Kingdom. Communicable Disease Report 1993; 3:R147-R152.
13. Guidelines for prevention of transmission of Human Immunodeficiency Virus and hepatitis B virus to health care and public workers., MMWR 1989; 38 (Suppl 6): 1-37.
14. Department of Health. Protecting health care workers and patients from hepatitis B, Recommendations of the advisory group on hepatitis. London: DOH, 1993 (August).
15. Kinnersly P. Attitudes of general practitioners towards their vaccination against hepatitis B. Br Med J 1990; 300: 238.
16. Morgan D R, Lamont T J, Dawson J D, Booth C. Decontamination of instruments and control of cross infection in general practice. Br Med J 1990; 300: 1379-80.
17. Foy C, Gallagher M, Rhodes T, et al. HIV and measures to control infection in general practice. Br Med J 1990; 300: 1048-9.
18. Brattebo G, Wisborg T, Sjursen H. Health workers and the human immunodeficiency virus: knowledge, ignorance and behaviour. Public Health 1990; 104: (2)123-30.
19. Sultan G. How much is known about HIV? London: Nursing 1991; 4(28): 14-7.
20. Sharp C, Maychell K, Walton I. Nursing and AIDS: material matters; issues, information and teaching materials on HIV and AIDS for nurses - a research study. National Foundation for Educational Research: Berkshire, 1993.
21. British Medical Association. A code of practice for the sterilisation of instruments and control of cross infection. London: BMA 1981.
22. British Medical Association, A code of practice for the safe use and disposal of sharps. London: BMA, 1990.
23. General Medical Services Committee. Minor surgery in general practice - a review. London: BMA 1994.

24. Minor surgery in general practice. Guidelines by the General Medical Services Committee and the Royal College of General Practitioners in collaboration with the Royal College of Surgeons of England, The Royal College of Surgeons of Edinburgh and the Joint Committee on Postgraduate training for General Practice. December 1991.
25. British Medical Association. Environmental and occupational risks of health care. London: BMA, 1994.

Chapter 3

Infection Control for District Nursing

Infection control and its application to nursing has primarily been associated with wards and departments in the hospital setting. Over recent years there has been a gradual change in the way that health care is delivered with a much greater emphasis being placed on care in the community. However, understanding the principles which govern infection control practice is a vital component of nursing practice regardless of the setting.

Robottom, Clarke and Chapple in 1981 stated district nursing "is concerned with people in their normal social setting, in their own homes with their families".[1] The district nurse is a guest in the patient's home and, therefore, does not have the same degree of environmental control as he or she would have in a hospital ward. The infection control issues which are particularly relevant to district nurses will be addressed in the chapter under the following headings:

· discharge and communication;
· the environment;
· handwashing;
· use and disposal of sharps;
· accidental inoculation;
· spillages of infected or potentially infected materials;
· protective clothing;
· laundry;
· clinical waste;
· specimens;
· equipment.

Discharge and Communication

Newman in 1991 advised that it is important to plan a discharge so that it "will anticipate a patient's community needs".[2] Knowing in advance of any issues which might compromise good infection control practice allows the district nurse to make suitable arrangements, providing continuity of care. At times discharges have to be hastily organised, for example when there is a shortage of beds. This in turn can result in certain details being overlooked. Such a detail may be the disposal of clinical waste for a patient who lives in a high-rise flat where difficulties in waste storage and disposal already exist.

Changes in clinical practice have sometimes made it difficult always to have suitable arrangements in place. Timoney suggested the ideal notice of a surgical patient returning to the community would be 48 hours, an impossible time frame for the increasing numbers of patients undergoing day surgery.[3]

Staff must be aware of the risks infection can pose to both patients and their families. District nurses need more information from hospital staff than simply the request to "assess" if continuity of care is to be achieved.

The Environment
....

Patients living in their own homes are not immune from acquiring infection and the district nurse must practice according to infection control principles in a wide variety of settings. Conditions will vary considerably and the patient's wishes must always be considered. For example, if a patient requests that a surface, such as a coffee table, is not used for laying out dressing materials and equipment then alternative arrangements must be made even if they may not prove to be as suitable. Whatever surface is used infection risks will be minimised if the principles of asepsis are followed.

Handwashing
....

Hands are important vehicles for the transfer of micro-organisms responsible for infection. Water, soap and towels are not necessarily as accessible as in a hospital ward. Some patients will provide a clean towel whilst others expect the nurses to supply their own. Paper towels can be left in the patient's home or carried by the nurse. A good handwashing technique is of prime importance, more so than the cleansing agent used or the length of time taken to wash the hands. The use of an alcohol-based hand rub is of particular value in homes where handwashing facilities are limited or not available.

Hands must be washed after the removal of gloves.[4]

Sharps
....

A sharp is defined as anything which is capable of puncturing the skin of the operator. Applying safe techniques in their use and disposal is essential. The person using the sharp is responsible for safely disposing it into the appropriate container. District nurses may carry a container for sharps disposal or leave a container in a patient's home. Leaving a container in the home must only be done after careful assessment. In the past containers carried by nurses in their own cars have tended to be on the large side and very visible when visiting a patient and there is also the added risk of spilling during transport. Small containers are now available.

Points in relation to safety are as follows:
- needles must never be re-sheathed as the risk of injury whilst holding the cap is high;[5]
- sharps containers should only be three-quarters full prior to sealing and disposal, they should be labelled to identify the source;
- sharps containers should not be placed in yellow sacks but kept separate during storage and transport;[6]
- all sharps containers must conform to British Standard 7320 and be readily available.[7]

Accidental Inoculation

Accidental inoculation includes:
- all penetrating sharps/needle injuries;
- contamination of lesions with blood or body fluids;
- scratches/bites involving broken skin (i.e. causing bleeding or visible puncture wound);
- splashes into eyes or mouth by blood or body fluids.

If an accident occurs encourage the wound to bleed and then wash with soap and water. Dry the area gently and if required cover with a waterproof dressing. Splashes to the conjunctiva should be irrigated with sterile saline or cold water. Splashes involving the mouth should be rinsed well with water which should then be spat out. The injured person should report the accident immediately and complete the necessary forms before attending the occupational health department. Each area should have a written policy for staff involved in such accidents, including those which occur outside normal working hours.

Spillage

Spillage of blood or body fluids in a patient's home is dealt with by wearing household gloves and a disposable apron. When dealing with blood spillage it is often advised[8] to use a hypochlorite solution of 10,000 ppm but as this cannot be used safely on all surfaces and in all circumstances, the use of hot water and detergent should be considered instead:
- as much fluid as possible should be absorbed using a disposable cloth or paper towels;
- the area should then be washed using detergent and hot water.

Protective Clothing

Aprons
There is some uncertainty as to when a disposable plastic apron should be worn during patient care. One of the purposes during patient care is to prevent the uniform or clothes, 'becoming soiled, moistened or stained', when carrying out nursing procedures.[9] It is advisable to wear a disposable apron when carrying out any procedure that may involve the likelihood of contamination by blood or body fluids.

Some district nurses now wear personal clothing; these should be washable.[10] However a plastic apron is still required.

Gloves
The use of well-fitting, non-sterile latex gloves are recommended when involved with any non-invasive patient care activity that can contaminate the hands with blood or body fluids. Gloves are also employed when cleaning equipment, handling disinfectants, cleaning spillage and for venepuncture in certain circumstances.[11] The use of vinyl gloves may be required by staff who are allergic to latex. Sterile gloves are not required except for certain aseptic procedures.

Laundry

Items which contain blood and body fluids can safely be washed in a washing machine on the hot cycle, following a cold cycle rinse. If such items need to be washed by hand household gloves should be worn.[11] For patients who do not possess a washing machine, arrangements may be made through the local authority. Always refer to local policies for arrangements on laundry.

Clinical Waste

This is a subject which creates much debate and discussion. Clinical waste is defined as, "any waste which consists wholly or partly of human or animal tissue, blood or other body fluids, excretions, drugs or other pharmaceutical products, swabs or dressings or syringes, needles or other sharp instruments, being waste which unless rendered safe may prove hazardous to any person coming into contact with it".[12]

There is very little guidance available on community clinical waste. Arrangements for collection of waste from private homes can normally be arranged with the local authority.

Clinical waste must not be transported by district nurses in their vehicles. Again always refer to local policy.

Collection and Transport of Specimens

It is important to transport specimens to the laboratory as quickly as possible.[13] Poor quality specimens give unreliable results.

Correct and meaningful information should be given on the request form and specimen container label. For example, when sending a wound swab, it is helpful to know the exact site and whether it is a surgical or non-surgical wound. If it is a surgical wound it is useful to state the nature of the operation, and whether the patient is pyrexial or receiving any relevant chemotherapy. If a specimen is for examination for viruses the date of onset of the illness should be stated.

All specimens are potentially hazardous therefore the specimen container must be placed in a sealable plastic bag. Staples or pins must not be used. The request form must be placed in the separate compartment.

The sealable plastic bag should then be placed in a durable 'metal or plastic container with a resealable lid'.[14] This container must be able to withstand being disinfected or autoclaved.[15]

Any specimen requiring mailing must be packaged in accordance with Post Office regulations to prevent leakage,[15] and subsequently placed in a plastic bag which is then put into a container, sealed with tape; the words 'Fragile with care-Pathological specimen' must be visible. First class letter post must be used.[14] A copy of the regulations are available from the Post Office.

Equipment for Patient Care

Whenever possible the use of disposable equipment is advised. Any items which are returned to a sterile supply department should be contained within a leak-proof resealable container, which is disposable or capable of being autoclaved.

Some units have a central equipment service for larger items that are collected from homes following use. These items may include commodes, chemical toilets, beds, mattresses and pressure relieving devices. Cleaning and decontamination is undertaken at a central point.

Each area will have its own guidance for the return of equipment that it to be re-used and it is advised to check what system is in operation.

For items of equipment that cause concern or where there is no agreed procedure, it is important to contact the local infection control team for advice.

Conclusion

This chapter has given guidance on infection control to district nurses that is based on safe practice in the prevention of infection.
Infection can be life threatening and cause a great deal of distress to the patient and their loved ones.

REFERENCES
1. Robottom B, Clark J, Chapple M. In: Baly ME, ed. Background to care in a new approach to district nursing. London: Heineman Medical Ltd, 1981.
2. Newman C. Receiving patients from hospital. In: Armitage SK, ed. Continuity of nursing care. London: Scutari Press, 1991.
3. Timoney R. A policy for community practice. J Infection Control Nursing/Nursing Times 1987; 83(9): 64-71.
4. Ayliffe G A J, Lowbury E J L, Geddes A M, Williams J D. Control of hospital infection: a practical handbook. 3rd ed. London: Chapman and Hall Medical, 1992.
5. British Medical Association. A code of practice for the safe use and disposal of sharps. London: BMA, 1990.
6. Health Services Advisory Committee. Safe disposal of clinical waste. London: HMSO, 1992; 6-41.
7. British Standards Institute. Specification for sharps containers. BS 7320. HCC/34, London: BSI, 1990.
8. Ayliffe G A J, Coates D, Hoffman P N. Chemical disinfection in hospitals. London: Public Health Laboratory Service, 1993.
9. Ayton M. Protective clothing - what do we use and when? J Infection Control Nursing/Nursing Times. 1984; 80(20): 68-70.

10. Walker A, Donaldson B. Dressing for protection. Nursing Times 1993; 89(2): 60-2.
11. Department of Health. Guidance for clinical health care workers: protection against infection with HIV and hepatitis viruses. Recommendations of the expert advisory group on AIDS. London: HMSO, 1990.
12. Health Services Advisory Committee. Safe disposal of clinical waste. London: HMSO, 1992. Appendix 1-18.
13. Ayliffe G A J, Lowbury E J L, Geddes A M, Williams J D. Control of hospital infection: a practical handbook. 3rd ed, London: Chapman and Hall Medical, 1992.
14. Public Health Laboratory Service. Safety precautions: notes for guidance. 4th ed. London, 1993.
15. Health Services Advisory Committee. Safe working and the prevention of infection in clinical laboratories. London: HMSO, 1991.

Dr J. K. Inman

Chapter 4

Infection Control in General Practice

Recent years have witnessed unprecedented changes to all aspects of health care as a result of many pressures including the health service reforms, increased litigation risk, media awareness and health and safety legislation. In addition, the struggle to tame nature continues with the battle against microbiological hazards. Pathogenic organisms have thrived as they evolve mechanisms to thwart man's best efforts to eliminate them by the latest antimicrobial agents. Traditional enemies of Man such as tuberculosis and diphtheria enjoy continuing resurgence as social conditions deteriorate abroad and, more worryingly, at home. Man's technological developments have unpredicted spin-offs, such as the potentially fatal contamination of the air-conditioning units in modern buildings with *Legionella*, or the unexpected importation to the UK of the malaria-carrying *Anopheles* mosquito via air travel. But probably the single most important factor to raise both public and professional interest in infection control has been the rise and spread of the Human Immunodeficiency Virus (HIV).

Since the early 1980s, when epidemiologists first recognised the clusters of opportunistic diseases affecting young homosexual men, knowledge of HIV and its spread has grown apace. The existence of a viral carrier state affecting otherwise apparently completely fit young adults precipitated a level of alarm throughout the western world which was so great that suddenly infection control became firmly on everyone's agenda. The World Health Organisation, Government departments of health and professional bodies all issued guidelines.[1, 2]

Coincidentally, the Health and Safety at Work etc. Act 1974 and the Control of Substances Hazardous to Health Act 1988 (COSHH) were also beginning to impact on all workplaces as it became a legal obligation for employers to take an active role in the identification, analysis and reduction of all identifiable workplace hazards,[3] thence to produce a specific written health and safety policy. As employers General Practitioners are, of course, subject to this legislation and therefore have to comply. In any case, common sense would suggest all health care workers should be fully aware of the dangers inherent in their profession and to follow best possible practice, but regrettably the few studies undertaken in recent times indicate a lamentable lack of knowledge of the risks or how to minimise them.[4, 5, 6]

The majority of contacts between health care workers and patients occur in general practice at an estimated rate of 750,000 patient consultations per day[6] so it seems strange that the majority of publications reflect the needs of hospitals. Probably the most useful publication to date for General Practitioners is the BMA code of practice.[7] The aim of the present paper is to provide an overview of the principal infective hazards in the general practice workplace to stimulate a continuing and more critical self assessment; it is not intended as a comprehensive treatise.

Health and Safety Policy
The initial stage in the development of any health and safety policy is the risk

assessment. For infection control, this assessment means the identification of infective health hazard, that is any micro-organism with pathogenic potential. Having identified the risk it must be considered in context and an assessment made. This principle covers all activities ranging from personal hygiene to the most complex of procedures. The concept of the universal precaution[8] has been developed, this is the assumption that all patients (regardless of diagnosis), and all medical staff and anything they handle have the potential to transmit infection of which they may or may not be aware.[9] The same precautions must be used for every patient. There are patients in the community who are more vulnerable to the less virulent infections, as for example the immunosuppressed who may be at risk from opportunistic organisms. The fungus which causes thrush, *Candida albicans*, is normally harmless but may become troublesome or even lethal as a result of the body's reduced defences. Thus it may be impossible to anticipate when an infection risk may occur.

The risk having been identified and an assessment made, the next stage is to decide what action is to be taken. This task may seem rather daunting when considering the wide range of activities which constitute general practice but when viewed systematically many problems are easily identified and solved. It is helpful to employ a computer analogy. The software variables are the tasks to be undertaken, the people involved and the systems they employ; and the hardware variables include the health centre, its design, the ergonomics of the workplace and the equipment available.

Straightforward protocols need to be devised and the general organisation must facilitate good practice. Because every surgery is unique, protocols appropriate to the patient profile and the types of procedures undertaken have to be drawn up and made available to all general practice staff.

The Patients, the Staff and the Procedures

Since the early days of Koch and Pasteur when the nature of the infectious agent was discovered, the fundamental importance of antisepsis and personal cleanliness as a means of combatting the spread of diseases has been well recognised. These basic principles are no less important today, even to the extent that many of the more modern developments in sterile technique may be simply undermined by an operator with contaminated fingers or clothing. The Victorians recognised the importance of simple yet effective improvements to general public health by promoting better housing, clean water supplies and sanitation, particularly for the poor, and one could argue that our modern consumer 'disposable-happy' society has allowed some of these principles to lapse. We have been lulled into a misguided sense of security.

The Potential for Cross Infection in the Surgery
Surgeries are settings with great potential for disease transmission to occur either from health care worker to patient, patient to health care worker or from patient to

patient. In its simplest form the risk might be that of catching a cold in the waiting room, but more sinister transmissions may occur which might not be recognised. Bacterial infections generally have a shorter incubation period than viral infections so a causal link is more easily established, as for example in the case of the common staphylococcal skin infection, impetigo. In contrast, viral incubation periods tend to be weeks, months or even years which may make the establishment of such connections very hard or even impossible.[7] In the event that the source is a health worker then the victims are more likely to be detected, but the likelihood of this diminishes the longer the incubation period.

In one example, fifty patients developed hepatitis B (HBV) after visiting a dermatologist[10] who was subsequently found to be HBsAg negative (i.e. not a carrier himself). In many ways a dermatology clinic is analogous to a general practitioner's surgery so this experience has direct relevance here. An epidemiological investigation concluded the possible sources of transmission to have been a contaminated electrocautery tip, repeated use of multidose vials of local anaesthetic, repeated use of cotton buds for liquid nitrogen and failure to wear gloves or wash hands properly when operating (interestingly the follow-up showed a number of patients to have had surgery after an HIV-positive patient had been operated on and yet none had evidence of having contracted HIV).

In a hepatitis A outbreak affecting patients in a burns unit[11] the most important risk factor was staff eating in the clinical area, also implicated was inadequate handwashing and subsequent oral contamination. Another outbreak[12] was traced to poor personal hygiene, including long fingernails and hand to mouth contact when drinking and smoking, in addition to handling contaminated faecal sample containers without gloves. Hepatitis A virus has been shown to survive for up to four hours on fingertips and can be transferred between fingertips and hard surfaces.[13]

One might argue that HIV or HBV are relatively rare in general practice and therefore less relevant infections. In contrast, very infective conditions such as the common cold or chicken pox are legion and they do cause a lot of suffering and absence from work and school. It is therefore important for general practice staff to be trained to employ instinctively and consistently the highest principles of personal hygiene and proper technique so as to minimise the chances of any cross infection. A useful concept is that of the 'dirty' and 'clean' area. Anything below table-top height is always to be regarded as dirty and all work surfaces should be predefined as clean or dirty. Children do put fingers on consulting room desks and staff often consume beverages in their rooms, neither of which are pleasant after a dirty MSU (urine) specimen bottle has been placed there by a previous patient!

Media attention has made much play on the possibility of infected health workers passing HIV onto patients. Reassuringly for the general public, no transmission occurred in a series of 19,000 patients treated by 57 HIV infected health care workers.[14] This seems to indicate that, provided infection control procedures are adhered to, transmission is very unlikely in a primary care situation. On current knowledge the risk of patients being infected by an HIV-positive health worker is estimated as less than 1:100 million. There is one recorded case, that of six patients who contracted HIV after visiting an infected Florida dentist.[15]

Of course if universal precautions are pursued to extreme there is a real possibility that certain patients may be neglected, either physically or psychologically, or even refused care altogether.[16] Thus the humanity, professionalism and common sense of the health worker are all important.

Prevention of Spread of Infection

It is well recognised that viruses can be transmitted by contaminated medical equipment[5] such as vaginal specula or tongue depressors and currently the most significant risks include hepatitis B, herpes simplex type 1, human papilloma virus, cytomegalovirus and tuberculosis.[6] The most effective means of preventing cross infection is to use disposable instruments where available, but financial constraints mitigate against this.[17] In addition there are those who feel that such use is environmentally profligate when one considers the enormous numbers of patient episodes involved, although arguably less so when compared with the 'cost' of managing cases of preventable HIV.

A few practices have standing arrangements with a local Central Sterile Supply Department (CSSD) for the regular supply of sterilised equipment[5] but most practices decontaminate their instruments in-house.

Currently the best method of sterilisation in general practice involves thorough precleaning[14] to remove all contaminants, followed by autoclaving, and it is important to remember that the decontamination of instruments should occur immediately after completion of the surgical procedure.[18] In certain circumstances less effective modes of instrument preparation are permitted, for example certain instruments such as thermometers will be damaged by heating and chemical disinfection with, for example, 70% alcohol for 10 minutes is acceptable. The important point to grasp is that the only truly effective way of eliminating bacterial spores is via the autoclave.[5] Unfortunately many doctors still misguidedly view a water boiler or kettle as a true steriliser. Disinfection (the inactivation of vegetative bacteria, viruses and fungi, but not necessarily of bacterial spores[5]) is acceptable in certain circumstances: for example in the cleaning of instruments for mucosal surface contact only, such as vaginal specula.

Procedures may be ranked into three main categories: high risk, medium risk and low risk, each having a minimum standard of decontamination. Unfortunately, the inappropriate use of these less effective techniques[4, 5, 6] continues to put patients at risk and would almost certainly result in successful litigation proceedings in the event of a significant mishap.

The ultimate responsibility for instrument cleaning rests with the partners in a practice, although the task is almost invariably performed by another member of the staff. Whoever does it, particularly members of the clerical or reception staff, must be properly instructed, for he or she may be put at risk by having no concept of the transmission of infection.

Most practitioners pay little attention to the less obvious infective hazards such as examination equipment. A study of auriscope earpieces[19] in use in general practices revealed almost a third to be contaminated with pathogenic bacteria; no doubt stethoscopes, patellar hammers and examination couches are all potential offenders also. The clinician's finger is often used in examination, gloves should always be worn when appropriate and a spatula used to examine the throat. Herpetic whitlows on the fingers are a well recognised hazard amongst certain health care workers.

Risks to the Health Care and Allied Workers

The greatest risk to the health care worker almost certainly occurs in the handling of sharps.[20] All contaminated needles and blades should be handled with utmost care and disposed of promptly into sharps bins.[21] These need to be readily accessible to reduce the likelihood of needles being passed around the room, thereby incurring the risk of needlestick injury. Roughly 40% of needlestick injuries occur at resheathing and no clinical glove will protect against a stab injury. The rate of seroconversion for HIV amongst health care workers who have sustained needlestick injury is 1:250.[22] In a series of 2000 cases of mucocutaneous exposure without skin or mucosal breaking no seroconversion occurred. There are a number of different specifications for sharps boxes, the best designs conform to the British Standards, but cost/benefit analysis often precludes the best option. Even the best sharps bin, if overfilled,[23] can be dangerous and needles can puncture the plastic wall.

Staff who perform clinical procedures need to be trained systematically to avoid hazard.[24] Hands should never be placed against a suture line and forceps should be used to retract or lift wound margins. Modern vacuum blood-taking equipment is safer than the traditional needle and syringe, but problems can occur if it is not used correctly or if patients are agitated or distressed.

Handling of Clinical Waste

Careless disposal of sharps also present the principal hazard to domestic and municipal workers when they handle waste. It is suggested that, to reduce the likelihood of inadvertent injury after any minor surgical procedure involving the use of sharps, clearing away should be the duty of the gloved operator and not an assistant who may be unaware of all the instruments used.

A recent study demonstrated a surprising degree of ignorance (or carelessness) about the disposal fate of different categories of waste and the colour coded bags.[25] Interestingly this has a cost implication as well as being important in infection control. In one hospital alone the inclusion of non-hazardous household waste in yellow bags resulted in an estimated extra one hundred bags labelled clinical waste at a cost of up to £100 per day! Thus all workers should understand and observe the local disposal policy.

In contrast to the alarming general media reports of syringes being washed up on coastal holiday resort beaches, the chances of the general public being affected by medical waste are actually very slim. But the trend of discharging patients from hospital to care in the community, and other sources of non-regulated medical waste (e.g. drug misusers or diabetics) may present increasing hazard to the general public. Obviously health care workers have an important role in educating patients. In the USA, any medical, laboratory or veterinary facility which produces over 50lbs per month of regulated medical waste is required to maintain detailed records and track waste from point of origin to final disposal.[26, 27]

Handling specimens prior to their despatch to the laboratory is an aspect which is often neglected. Unless there is both a designated reception point and subsequent handling procedure, non-clinical staff and visitors to the health centre may be at risk. In particular, areas where food or beverages are consumed may become contaminated. In addition, patients are inclined to present their samples for testing by placing them on the desk in the course of a consultation so it is appropriate to educate patients to keep samples out of consulting rooms or always put them directly on the floor rather than a clean desk top.

It is important to be aware that, although modern detergents have allowed the energy-saving trend of low temperature clothes washing to develop in recent years, a high temperature wash is often necessary to properly decontaminate clothing.

Gloves and Protective Clothing

The wearing of gloves is recommended for certain procedures. In 1987 the Royal College of Obstetricians and Gynaecologists advised thin disposable polythene type gloves to be inadequate for gynaecological and family planning procedures.[28] Many doctors and nurses now use latex gloves exclusively. Staff should always wear gloves when handling faecal samples which have been proven to cause cross infection.[12]

Face masks, protective glasses and aprons should also be available for clinical procedures and cleaning of dirty equipment. Cleaning dirty equipment requires special attention to hygiene, for a scrubbing action can produce an aerosol type spray and contamination of clothing, shoes and skin, and thereby transfer of pathogens.

Accidents and Spillages

Accidents happen and all staff should be aware of the simple yet crucial principles to deal with any anticipated risk. Surgeries should all follow recognised protocols,[7] the principal risks being those of spillage and sharps injury.

Spillages of any biological fluid or specimen should be subject to the same universal precaution, the application of hypochlorite as solution or granules.[6] It is known that HBV can survive for some time in dried blood so prompt and correct action is paramount. Where contamination of a mucous membrane or broken skin has occurred then this should be treated as a needlestick injury. For spills on to intact skin soap and water is the agent of choice.

Immunisations

Immunisation of all staff who come in direct contact with the patient or blood specimens is now recommended and this should take into account not only the risk of the health worker contracting disease, e.g. hepatitis B or tuberculosis, but also the danger of transmission to the vulnerable patient, e.g. rubella.

Use of Antibiotics

There has been concern about the inappropriate use of antibiotics by many professionals, including doctors, veterinary surgeons and even farmers. This may lead to increasing resistance to antibiotics in the community[29, 30] and consequent difficulty in managing infections. For this reason antibiotics should not be used casually and patients need to be educated as to a realistic expectation of treatment for trivial conditions such as self-limiting viral sore throats. One might argue that the use of the newer antibiotics should be restricted so as to maintain their efficacy. Many new antibiotics are promoted by glossy advertisements aimed at the gullible, but antibiotic use should be based on a working knowledge of the different types and their actions against specific types of organism, for example atypical infections and tetracyclines. Hospital clinicians already have evidence of the adaptive skills of bacteria with the appearance of 'superbugs' such as multiple resistant *Staphylococcus aureus* (MRSA). So an antibiotic policy must be an important component of any infection control regime.

Health Centre Design and Specification of Equipment

It is not within the scope of this article to cover health centre specifications but a few observations are relevant. Few general practitioners have the good fortune to be able to build their own surgery and ideally the design should take into account the anticipated ergonomics of the practice. Advice might be obtained from a local infection control officer.

The waiting area should allow the segregation of infectious patients, either scheduled or unannounced, and, in common with all the patient access areas, should have easily cleaned floor coverings, upholstery and work surfaces. The toilet facilities should also be adequate and easy to maintain.

The clinical areas should be well organised and the areas for clean and dirty procedures clearly defined and arranged to reduce cross-contamination; all too often in many health centres the handling and cleaning of contaminated equipment or specimens takes place near or across a clean area.

The correct methods, equipment and chemicals for cleaning, sterilising and storing clinical instruments in accordance with current best accepted practice should be specified and always easily available. Sterilisation equipment should itself be properly serviced and safely sited.

Summary
The COSHH regulations oblige employers to provide a health and safety policy statement. This involves a complete workplace assessment of risks and control measures,[31] with appropriate information, training and supervision of staff. As employers, general practitioner principals are required by law to conform and may be subject to inspection visits from the Health & Safety Executive; general practitioners are also professionals and their insistence on conscientious adherence to infection control is paramount in ensuring the confidence of patients, and acknowledging the rights of general practice staff and their families at home.

A good infection control policy will cover all the aspects alluded to in the text - basic hygiene, instrument cleaning, maintenance of decontamination equipment, handling of toxic materials and waste disposal. Straightforward procedures should be devised and the general organisation must facilitate good practice, but above all these protocols should be owned by all the staff.

The most potent weapon in the fight against infection is knowledge. If all health professionals understand the principles of infection control and are involved in the specification of any health and safety policy, then they will be well motivated to practise their routines in a safe and confident manner.

REFERENCES
1. Levin A C, Gums J G, Grauer K. Tuberculosis, the primary care physician's role in eradication. Postgrad Med 1993; 93(3): 46-50,53-60.
2. Social Services Committee. Problems associated with AIDS. Vol.1. Report together with proceedings of Committee. London: HMSO, 1987.
3. Health and Safety Executive. A step-by-step guide to COSHH assessment. London, 1993.
4. Foy C, Gallagher M, Rhodes T, et al. HIV and measures to control infection in general practice Br Med J 1990; 300: 1048-9.
5. Hoffman P M, Cooke E M, Larkin D P, et al. Control of infection in general practice: a survey and recommendations, Br Med J 1988: 297: 34-6.
6. Morgan D R, Lamont T J, Dawson J D, Booth C. Decontamination of instruments and control of cross infection in general practice: Br Med J 1990; 300: 1379-80.
7. BMA. A code of practice for the sterilisation of instruments and control of cross infection. London: British Medical Association, 1989.
8. Leads from the Morbidity Mortality Weekly Report. Update: Universal precautions for prevention of transmission of Human Immunodeficiency Virus, hepatitis B virus and other blood borne pathogens in health-care settings. JAMA 1988; 260(4): 462-5.
9. Mosley J W. Virus transmission in health care settings. Precautions, epidemiologic experience & common sense. Am J Public Health 1993; 83(12): 1664-5.
10. Hlady W G, Hopkins R S, Ogilby T E, Allen S T. Patient-to-patient transmission of hepatitis B in a dermatology practice. Am J Public Health 1993; 83(12): 1689-93.
11. Doebbeling B N, Li N, Wenzel R P. An outbreak of hepatitis A among Health Care Workers : Risk factors for transmission. Am J Public Health 1993; 83: 1679-84.
12. Rosenblum L S, Villarine M E, Nainan O V, et al. Hepatitis A outbreak in a neonatal intensive care unit: risk factors for transmission and evidence of prolonged viral excretion among preterm infants. J Infect Dis 1991; 164(3): 476-82.
13. Mbithi J N, Springthorpe V S, Boulet J R, Sattar S A. Survival of hepatitis A virus on human hands and its transfer on contact with animate and inanimate surfaces. J Clin Microbiol 1992; 30(4): 757-63.
14. Hammond L. Office sterilisation. Aust Fam Physician 1990; 19(5): 693.
15. Robinson P, Challacombe S. Transmission of HIV in a dental practice - the facts. Br Dent J 1993; 175(10):383-4.
16. Molinari J A. HIV, health care workers and patients - how to ensure safety in the dental office. J Am Dent Assoc 1993; 124(10): 51-6.
17. DiGiacamo J C, Odom J W, Ritota P C, Swan K G. Cost containment in the operating room; use of reusable versus disposable clothing. Ann Surg 1992; 58(10): 654-6.
18. Crow S. Protecting patients, personnel, instruments in the OR. AORN J 1993; 58(4): 771-4.
19. Overend A, Hall W W, Godwin P G. Does earwax lose its pathogens on your auriscope overnight? Br Med J 1992; 305: 1571-3.
20. (Needlestick injury) Advisory Committee on Dangerous pathogens. LSAV/HTLVIII - The Causative agent of AIDS & related conditions. Revised guidelines. Lancaster: DHSS, 1986.
21. Gwyther J. Sharps disposal containers and their use. J Hosp Infect 1990; 15(3): 287-94.
22. Scully C, Porter S R. Can HIV be transmitted from dental personnel to patients by dentistry? Br Dent J 1993; 175(10): 381-2.
23. McGovern K. Some pointers on needle safety. Nursing 1986; 16(10): 58-9.
24. Cooper C W. Prevention of HIV and HBV transmission in general practice. Med J Aust 1993; 159(5): 339-42.
25. Beaumont G. Bad riddance to rubbish. Journal of Infection Control Nursing Nursing Times 1992; 88(14): 63-4.
26. Lichtveld M Y, Rodenbeck S E, Lybarger J A. The findings of the agency for toxic substances & disease Registry Medical Waste Tracking Act Report, Environ Health Perspect 1992; 98: 243-50.
27. Environmental Protection Agency. Standards for tracking & management of medical waste. Federal Register: 1989; 54: 12326-95.
28. Royal College of Obstetricians and Gynaecologists. Problems associated with AIDS in relation to Obstetrics and Gynaecology. London: RCOG, 1987.
29. Hammond L. Antibiotic resistance in general practice. Aust Fam Physician 1990; 19(5): 723-4, 727, 730-1.
30. Haddy R I, Doughman L A, Elder B L, Markert R J. Cefoxitin induced antibiotic resistance in Enterobacter species in the community hospital. Fam Pract Res J 1992; 12(3): 305-12.
31. Health & Safety Executive. Working with Employers. London: HSE 26.

Mr Mike V. Martin

Chapter 5

Infection Control in Dentistry

The practice of dentistry is conducted in a part of the body where there is high potential for cross infection. Most dental procedures involve the release of blood which together with saliva are known to transmit infection to health care workers.[1, 2] Viruses such as hepatitis B and herpes type 1 are known to be spread by dental procedures.[3] It was however the emotive problem of the spread of Human Immunodeficiency Virus (HIV) that prompted dental professional organisations worldwide to formulate guidelines on infection control. Most of these guidelines when originally formulated were almost unworkable and compliance was poor. Increasing knowledge of HIV and its transmission have allowed British infection control guidelines to be rewritten and more applicable to routine dental procedures. [4, 5, 6]

The present infection control guidelines in dentistry are based on a simple single standard that is applicable to all patients. This single standard of infection control is safe for known or unknown carriers of infectious disease. The essential elements of the infection control guidelines are personal protection, sterilization, disinfection and safe waste disposal.

Personal Protection

It is important that all the dental team understand how infectious disease could be transmitted in dentistry. This knowledge together with the techniques used should be regularly audited so that a consistently high standard is achieved. Auditing by regular observation or meetings allows the correction of poor or unsafe techniques, in addition to reinforcing the importance of infection control.

All personnel should receive and be up to date with immunisations against known infectious disease.[7] Table 1 illustrates the vaccination schedule recommended for those involved in dentistry. All of the vaccinations are important but the hepatitis B vaccine is vital as this virus is known to be spread in dentistry by accidental

Table 1
Vaccination Scedule for Dental Personnel

	Route	Length of Protection/ Comments
Tetanus	IM	10 years
Poliomyelitis	Oral	Probably infectious for up to 6 weeks after vaccination
Hepatitis B	IM	3-5 years
Tuberculosis	Intradermal	Test if no Mantoux or BCG dose in childhood
Rubella (for female)	IM	Lifelong

inoculation with infected saliva or blood. The serum antibody concentration must be maintained above 100 IU and retesting is recommended every three years.

Infection Control Techniques

It is essential to wear protective materials during dental procedures, these include gloves, masks, glasses and long-sleeved surgery coats.

Gloves must be worn during all dental procedures. These protect the patient from infection present on the operator's hands. Gloves also protect the operator from micro-organisms present in the patient's mouth. Studies have looked at the integrity of gloves during dental procedures.[8] The consensus of opinion is that gloves are liable to puncture and therefore must be changed after each patient. For most operative procedures a good quality non-sterile glove can be used which is washed using a systematic method prior to the start of treatment and discarded afterwards. It is important to wash the hands prior to donning gloves to reduce the transient micro-flora.

The increased use of gloves by dental personnel has been accompanied by an increase in 'allergy' to gloves. In practice this is, in the majority of dental personnel, not 'allergy' but irritant contact dermatitis.[9] The regular changing of gloves, the use of a careful handwashing technique with good rinsing and drying of the hands will solve many problems.[10] Further prevention of irritant contact dermatitis can be achieved by the regular use of a proprietary hand cream which prevents drying and cracking of the epithelium. Simple methods are described in the article by Field and her colleagues[11] which can prevent most irritant contact dermatitis. If true allergic dermatitis is present then the help of a consultant dermatologist should be sought. The use of gloves in dentistry is quite different to that in most branches of surgery. Gloves are worn almost continuously five days every week for 45-50 weeks a year. It would be expected that the use of gloves and hand disinfectants would in time cause selection of disinfectant-resistant flora on the hands, this does not appear to happen.[12]

Masks are strongly recommended to be worn during all operative procedures. This is not a protection against aerosols but to protect against the splattering of saliva and coolant liquids during operative procedures. Most masks become permeable to micro-organisms during operative procedures. There is still considerable controversy as to whether aerosols are an infection risk in dentistry; the available evidence is still equivocal.[13, 14]

Glasses are essential for all dental personnel during operative procedures. They protect operators against traumatic injuries to the eye (e.g. amalgam or tooth debris) which can occur quite frequently. They also protect against splattering of the eyes by saliva, blood or other organic detritus. Transconjunctival passage of hepatitis B has been reported during dental procedures[15] and the potential for herpes type 1 infection is always present. Protective or prescription glasses do need to be cleaned with soap and water between patients.

Clean long-sleeved gowns are necessary for dental surgery. For non-invasive procedures they do not need to be sterile or to be changed after every patient. It is essential for them to have long sleeves to protect the arms from splatter.

Sterilization

Dental instruments have undergone a major revolution in the last few years and now most are sterilizable or disposable. The preferred method for sterilization is by autoclaving. The use of cold chemical or hot air sterilization is not recommended as both are unreliable. The use of a combined chemical and heat sterilizer is also not recommended since the chemicals used are potentially carcinogenic and if they escape from the device would exceed the occupational exposure limits prescribed by Control of Substances Hazardous to Health Act 1988 (COSHH 1989).[16]

Three processes are necessary for sterilization, these are presterilization cleaning, sterilization and aseptic storage. Presterilization is best achieved by use of an ultrasonic bath. Ultrasonic baths are effective and efficient; they are best filled with a liquid detergent and water which must be regularly changed. Hand cleaning of instruments, if done, should employ a brush with heavy duty gloves being worn to prevent sharp injuries. Holding baths filled with detergent or detergent and disinfectant combinations are useful if instruments are heavily blood contaminated. After cleaning the instruments are sterilized by autoclaving. The last few years have seen the manufacture of a plethora of different autoclaves with a variety of holding times; the recommended holding times are shown in Table 2.

Table 2
Temperature and Time Combinations for Autoclave

Temp °C	Holding Time (mins.)
134-138	3
126-129	10
121-124	15
115-118	30

Most instruments in dentistry are amenable to sterilization by autoclaving, one possible exception is dental slow speed handpieces (drills) or high speed turbines. It has been claimed that these handpieces are deleteriously affected by autoclaving.

If handpieces are carefully externally cleaned with soap and water and then oiled with a high quality oil then the damage from autoclaving can be reduced. It is essential that these rotary instruments are sterilized between patients as there is evidence that viruses can be aspirated into the turbine head and water lines and remain viable.[17]

Disinfection

Disinfectants are used in dentistry for surfaces. Disinfectants should not be used for instruments that can be autoclaved.

The danger of infection from surfaces contaminated with blood or saliva would appear to be small. There have been no reported cases of infection from surgery surfaces. A disinfectant is useful for the treatment of contaminated surfaces, but more important is the thorough cleaning of the area and dilution of potential pathogens. Most opportunistic pathogens require a minimal infective dose to cause an infection. It is important that the areas that are being touched by the surgery operators are identified. This concept, which is called zoning, allows the identification of the areas to be cleaned and disinfected and, therefore, throughput of patients.

Surface disinfectants are multitudinous in variety and properties. They should be effective, inexpensive, user friendly, have good shelf life and not contravene the COSHH regulations.[16]

The spittoon and aspirator systems should be cleaned and disinfected before and after every treatment session. A disinfectant containing 10,000 ppm of available chlorine should be used.

Waste Disposal

There is a statutory duty for all dentists to dispose of contaminated waste in a safe manner. In practice this means disposal by incineration or at a registered deep landfill site. Contaminated waste should be placed in a clinical waste bag overprinted with the words 'Danger of Infection' with the source indicated. Similarly sharps should be placed in a 'sharps box' which must not be more than two-thirds full. Clinical waste and sharps boxes must be stored in a place where there is no public access and where they will not be punctured.

REFERENCES
1.   Levin M L, Maddrey W C, Wands J R, Mendeloff A L. Hepatitis B transmission by dentists. JAMA 1974; 228(9): 1139-40.
2.   Rimland D, Parkin W E, Miller G B, Schrack W D. Hepatitis B outbreak traced to an oral surgeon. N Engl J Med 1977; 296(17): 953-8.
3.   Manzella J P, McConville J H, Valenti N. An outbreak of herpes simplex virus type 1 gingivostomatitis in a dental hygiene practice. JAMA 1984; 252(15): 2019-22.
4.   Glenwright H D, Martin M V. Infection control in dentistry a practitioners guide. Occasional Paper No. 2. London: British Dental Association, July 1993.
5.   Martin M V. Infection control in the dental environment. Effective procedures. London: Martin Dunitz, 1991.
6.   Wood P. Cross infection control in dentistry. A practical guide. London: Wolfe Publications, 1991.
7.   Department of Health. Immunisation against infectious disease. London: HMSO, 1992.
8.   Burke F J, Wilson N H, Cheung S W. Glove use by dentists in England and Wales: results of a two-year follow-up survey. Br Dent J 1994; 176(9): 337-41.
9.   Field E A, King C M. Skin problems associated with routine wearing of protective gloves in dental practice. Br Dent J 1990; 169(9): 281-5.
10. Field E A. Hand hygiene, hand care and hand protection for clinical dental practice. Br Dent J 1994; 176(4): 129-34.
11. Field E A, Jedynakiewicz N M, King C M. A practical gloving and handwashing regimen for dental practice. Br Dent J 1992; 172(3): 111-13.
12. Millns B, Martin M V, Field E A. An investigation of chlorhexidine and cetyl pyridinum chloride resistant flora of dental students and theatre staff. J Hosp Infect 1994; 26: 99-104.
13. Orr N W. Is a mask necessary in the operating theatre? Ann R Coll Surg Engl 1981; 63(6): 390-2.
14. Craig D C, Quayle A A. The efficacy of face masks. Br Dent J 1985; 158(3): 87-90.
15. Kew M C. Possible transmission of serum (Australia-antigen-positive) hepatitis via the conjunctiva. Infect Immun 1973; 7(5): 823-4.
16. Occupational Exposure Limits. Guidance note EH40/89. London: Health and Safety Executive, 1989.
17. Lewis D L, Arens M, Appleton S S, et al. Cross-contamination potential with dental equipment. Lancet 1990; 340: 1252-4.

Ms Val Leggett

Chapter 6

Infection Control within Mental Healthcare Environments

Introduction

C are of mental health clients demands special attention and some of the aspects of this can be outside the usual scope of infection control. To date, there has been little research into the potential problems of infection control within mental healthcare areas and so this chapter includes personal experience.

The various international prevalence surveys of nosocomial infection rates have to date excluded mental healthcare areas. There are no United Kingdom infection statistics involving mental health clients to assist with infection control service planning within specialist mental healthcare environments.

Mental illness accounts for approximately 14% of NHS inpatient costs and 14% of certified sickness absence. The Health of the the Nation White Paper[1] details five main key areas for future activities, one of the primary targets being "To improve significantly the health and social functioning of mentally ill people".

Infection control can greatly assist with achieving this target by training staff on infection and hygiene matters with the intention of improving general conditions for the client and providing information which can in turn be related to this vulnerable client group.

It is my experience that currently 'long stay' mental healthcare facilities place the greatest demand upon the infection control nurse's time in terms of practical infection control interventions. A few prevalence surveys of nosocomial infection rates in USA long term care facilities for the elderly have revealed rates of approximately 15%. These studies have resulted in the suggestion that the rates equate to every resident having one infection per year. However, statistics should be treated with some caution as the average age of the population studied was 85 years .[2, 3, 4]

Practical infection control can be made extremely difficult by the behaviour and communication difficulties of some mental health clients. The principles of infection control are undoubtedly the same for any healthcare environment, but the practices to achieve the desired control in mental health facilities may require some creativity. Mental healthcare policy developments of the last 35 years have resulted in many 'Asylums' closing, and new care facilities/services being created. In the future, developments within mental healthcare environments will involve the creation of diverse care establishments as well as catering for increasingly 'mobile' clients. Infection control personnel should be involved with the design and planning of the new healthcare facilities.

Infection control advisers should adopt a client centred approach which will take into account unique facets of each client's social behaviour and mental state. If practical infection control is solely dependent upon the individual client's comprehension of, and compliance with, nursing advice, then there might be a high failure rate and infection may spread to other clients.

Mental healthcare Services within the UK are provided within a variety of environments[5] with their own inherent risks. These may include:

- the client's own home;
- day hospitals, day centres, drop-in centres, community health/resource centres;
- crisis accommodation, group homes/flatlets, adult placement schemes;
- private or voluntary residential care homes;
- hospital acute wards for disturbed, suicidal or especially vulnerable people;
- hospital long stay wards;
- secure units, medium secure (forensic psychiatry) units (patients referred by special hospitals, courts, prisons and local services);
- high security units (special hospitals).

Infection Control Considerations

Mental health clients admitted for specialist care can coincidentally have a wide range of medical problems. Breaks in the skin due to self-injurious behaviour, sores or ulcerative conditions are not uncommon. One study on self-injurious behaviour revealed that three-quarters of a (learning difficulties) hospital population were without expressive language and most injured themselves more than once a day; the most common forms of self-injurious behaviour being cited as head banging, self biting and self scratching.[6]

Wound care can be a challenge when clients have phobic tendencies or if they persistently interfere with dressings as in the case of repetitive self interference. Auto-infection and delayed healing for such clients is a real possibility. The sites of some self-inflicted wounds can lead to difficulties with wound care, e.g. genitalia. Few generalisations can be offered as each client is unique. However, it is worth remembering that depressed clients may be mentally incapable and physically incapable of caring for themselves so personal hygiene may be poor. The link between immunosuppression and stress is now recognised. Clients admitted for mental healthcare may be highly stressed and particularly susceptible to the acquisition of infection or reactivation of infection such as varicella-zoster virus (shingles). Clients who require assistance as a result of alcohol, substance abuse or drug misuse may have engaged in unsafe behaviour associated with high risk of blood-borne infection. On admission to hospital, some clients may be in a malnourished and neglected state, a recent survey of London's homelessness hostels suggest that 30% of homeless men and 60% of homeless women have serious mental health problems.[7]

Clients with learning disabilities may have coexisting physical problems, and/or problems due to lower than normal personal hygiene or unusual behaviour, examples being coprophagia, a tendency to bite or a habit of eating soil or grass. Many such patients have a specific medical syndrome of which mental retardation is only one part. Examples of such syndromes are Down's syndrome (approximately 50% have cardiac defects), Arnold-Chiari malformation, Hurler syndrome, Hurler-Sheie, Sanfillipo and Sly syndromes.[8] Immunosuppression can accompany these syndromes. Mouth ulceration/bleeding gums have been observed to be side effects of some anti-epileptic medications. Such side effects can present a serious cross infection hazard if the client is wont to bite staff and other patients.

People with learning disabilities can, occasionally, be symptomless carriers of pathogenic micro-organisms, which places special obligations on those responsible for caring for them. It is known that Down's syndrome patients are more likely to be symptomless carriers of such infections as hepatitis B. Research published in 1984 described the blood screening for markers of hepatitis B infection of 2,239 people with learning difficulties and the result revealed 5.5% were carriers of hepatitis B e antigen.[9]

A study by Follett leads to the conclusion that there are major demographic differences in infection rates for this client group.[10]

In 1993 22,100 people with learning disabilities/mental handicap were living in longstay hospitals. In December 1992 a national conference 'Health sexuality : HIV and people with learning difficulties' sought to remind healthcare workers that this group may be sexually active. The same is the case in psychiatric care areas where some clients may lack ordinary inhibitions; some infection control staff participate in training/counselling on safer sex techniques as part of their infection control role.

A popular misconception is that intravenous drug misusers care little about infection risks. The success of needle exchange schemes and the experience of staff involved with harm reduction indicates that most clients worry about infection risks and actively seek assistance.[11]

Mental Healthcare Accommodation/Activities

A Salmonella food poisoning outbreak (240 people) which occurred at the Stanley Royd Hospital in 1984,[12] demonstrated the severe potential of infection spread within the old 'Asylum' type buildings, traditionally used to accommodate long stay, mentally ill people. Such buildings are large with difficult to clean environments and limited facilities for staff and patient handwashing.

The Patients Charter has placed demands for improved facilities for patient privacy but single room accommodation can still be in limited supply and, often, mental health clients in long stay areas cannot easily cope with being moved out of their room to accommodate somebody needing isolation due to infection. A general feature of long stay clients is that they tend to accumulate more possissions than patients in general hospitals and the hoarding of food (and other substances) in lockers and wardrobes can pose an infection control problem.

Long stay areas function as patients' homes, work and recreation centres contained within a relatively small geographic area. In the event of highly transmissible, respiratory spread infection (e.g. chickenpox) the infection control nurse tracing the client's close contacts will find that they may have travelled throughout the total area and will have associated with clients and staff from most ward areas. Group activities and crowding have been cited to be a major cause of nosocomial infection in long term care areas for the elderly; the incidence of nosocomial pneumonia being possibly as high as 70-115 patients per 1,000 per year.[3]

Therapeutic activities such as horticulture, farming, industrial therapies utilising visual stimulatory equipment/soft play equipment or food handling may require some assessment and advice from the infection control nurse. Hydrotherapy pools used by people with learning disabilities/severe mental health problems may be subject to a higher rate of accidental contamination than pool areas within general hospitals. Hydrotherapy pool management arrangements may include fresh chlorine dosing or total draining and cleaning of the pool.

Patients' launderettes and washing machines provided on wards for patients' use or on site Personal Clothing Laundries should be an area of interest/intervention for the infection control nurse.

The suitability of location/accommodation used for therapeutic pets and birds should be carefully considered by infection control personnel. It is advisable for written policies to be drafted detailing the management of the pet's health, food storage and feeding area, safe handling and disposal of excreta.

Source Isolation Precautions.
Single Room Isolation Dilemmas

In a general hospital a standard approach to the actual location of sharps disposal containers, protective gloves and aprons is for sites to be chosen as near as possible to the numerous points of actual use. This principle is not so easily applied within mental healthcare areas where it is essential that all sharps boxes are removed after individual use to a locked clinical room environment, i.e. away from patients. Likewise, protective clothing should be sited in locked or observed areas. I know of one patient who ate plastic aprons! Learning disability clients and suicidal patients must not be able to gain access to plastic disposal bags; consequently the location of clinical waste bins needs careful selection.

Single room isolation or cohort nursing of clients with infection can occasionally be a problem. Some 'Nightingale' wards do not have single rooms or small dormitory areas. Occasionally total ward isolation is necessary when there is a possibility that other clients may be incubating an infection.

Isolation/containment of the client may be severely detrimental to their mental state or the client may not co-operate and wander. Other clients may fail to comprehend that they should not enter the isolation room. Various coping strategies can be adopted to cope with these problems.

Conclusions

Infection control nurses employed within mental healthcare areas will need to apply their knowledge in three quite different care environments, i.e. the community setting, acute psychiatric ward environments and long stay care facilities. Long stay care facilities require clear systems for recognition and reporting of infection supported by audit, infection surveillance and ongoing training programmes.[13]

The key to successful infection control is the ability to improve knowledge of the subject and influence infection control. All staff should view themselves as health educators. Once provided with an up-to-date knowledge of infection and hygiene this will inevitably benefit clients and their carers. The infection control nurse should act as an information resource to all healthcare staff and inspire a commitment to preventing infection.

REFERENCES
1. Department of Health. Health of the nation. London: DOH, 1993.
2. Smith P W. The relevance of infection control programmes in long term facilities. Proceedings of the Third International Conference on Infection Control ICNA, 1992: 81-7.
3. Smith P W. Nosocomial infections in the elderly. Infect Dis Clin North Am 1989; 3(4): 763-77.
4. Bentley D W, Cheney L. Infection control in the nursing home: The physician's role. Geriatrics 1990; 45(11): 59-66.
5. Department of Health. Health of the nation. Key Area Handbook - Mental Illness. London: DOH, 1993.
6. Emberson J, Walker K. Self-injurious behaviour in people with a mental handicap. Nursing Times 1990; 86(23): 43-6.
7. Keating F, et al. Homelessness and mental health initiative - one year on. London: The Sainsbury Centre for Mental health Studies, 1992.
8. Katz J, Benumof J L, Kadis L B. Anaesthesia and uncommon diseases. 3rd ed. Philadelphia: WB Saunders Co, 1990.
9. Clarke S K, Caul E O, Jancar J. Gordon-Russell JB. Hepatitis B in seven hospitals for the mentally handicapped. J Infect; 1984; 8(1): 34-43.
10. Follett E. Mental Homes: a special risk? Occupational Health 1987: 51-52.
11. Holmes R, Waller T. Hepatitis C: time to wake up. Drug Link 1993 (May/June).
12. Department of Health and Social Security. The Report of the Committee of Inquiry into an Outbreak of Food Poisoning at Stanley Royd Hospital. London: HMSO, 1986.
13. Murdoch S. A safe environment for care: Infection Control nurses' role in mental health units. Prof Nurse 1992; 7(8): 519-22.

Mrs Sue Ross

Chapter 7

Infection Control in Childcare Facilities

Day care facilities for children are believed to have been available since the early 1800s. It has been suggested[1] that its growth in today's climate has been influenced by such social and economic factors as:

· increased proportion of single parent families;
· growth in divorce rate;
· mothers wishing to establish or continue professional careers;
· awareness of equal opportunities;
· increased number of extended families.

Approximately 28% of women in Britain with children under 5 years of age go to work compared with 50% in France and 75% in Belgium.[2]

Family disruption and economic loss may occur if parents have to take time off work to look after a sick child and it is therefore important that measures are taken to reduce the risk of infections occurring in day care settings through the implementation of "basic common-sense" infection control policies.[3]

Families with young children have varying needs for educational and day care facilities. All the facilities should provide young children with a clean, safe and healthy environment. Equally important, children should have quality day care, facilitated by trained workers in order to achieve standards of healthy child development.[4]

The principal types of child day care in the United Kingdom include:

· local authority and independent day nurseries; these provide full day care all year round;
· playgroups; provide sessional care for children between two and a half and five years;
· private nursery schools; offer educational and day care facilities, usually within school term times;
· nursery units of independent schools usually provide early access to the school;
· maintained nursery schools and classes; these are establishments with their own legal identity, but are integral parts of primary schools;
· primary schools; with under fives reception classes;
· combined nursery centres; which are overseen by local education authority and local authority social services departments. They take children from 18 months to 5 years;
  child minders; who work in domestic premises (usually their own homes) and offer full day care all year round;

Factors Influencing the Spread of Infection in Day Nurseries

There are a number of factors which aid the transmission of infectious agents in a day care setting. These include the prevalence of the agent in the population represented and the number of susceptible children[5], the age of the children and the standard of hygiene practised by staff.

Children who attend day care are particularly susceptible to infectious diseases for several reasons. These have been identified[6] as being:
- young age and subsequent immature immune system;
- the degree of close contact between the children;
- lack of hygiene practices, possibly due to age and lack of understanding;
- lack of prior encounters with micro-organisms;
- ambulatory status;
- incomplete immunizations and decreasing maternally acquired antibodies;
- the behavioural characteristics of children, that is their natural intimacy with others and exploratory behaviour favours the exchange of secretions and hand to mouth transmission of infection;
- bites and abrasions are common portals of entry for pathogens.

Infection Control Precautions

The Environment

Day nurseries should always provide a warm, light, welcoming environment. There is no doubt that environmental factors can play a major role in the spread of micro-organisms[7]. It is important that interventions are employed to minimise these risks. Facilities for children under two years of age are required to fulfil certain criteria. These include several which will aid the control of infection; for example the need for separate rooms for babies and toddlers.

The sharing of equipment, such as highchairs and toys, increases the risk of the transmission of infection.[6] These objects can become contaminated through handling or children putting their mouths to them. Toys should be washed in hot soapy water and dried thoroughly on a regular basis and immediately if obviously contaminated. Soft toys can be washed in a washing machine.

During an outbreak of diarrhoea and vomiting, water and sand play should cease as the potential for faecal/oral transmission is increased.

Nurseries should have a written cleaning schedule detailing the areas for cleaning, the frequency and the agents to be used.

Special attention should be paid to high risk areas such as toilets and kitchens. It is important that such schedules are monitored, evaluated and revised as necessary.

In a survey of six day-care centres swabs were taken for culture from surfaces and objects in the classroom and bathroom,[8] including swabs from toilet seats, toilet flush handles, potty chairs and toys. The results showed that a clear policy for cleaning environmental surfaces was essential for controlling the spread of infection. Chorba *et al.* [9] emphasised the importance of using a dedicated nappy changing area, with easily cleaned impervious surfaces, as changing mats can become contaminated and act as reservoirs for enteric micro-organisms.

It is recognized that the basic protective clothing required, when dealing with incidents where contact with body fluid is anticipated, is a disposable plastic apron and a pair of disposable latex gloves,[10] Bonner and Dale,[11] examining the incidence of giardiasis in children from day care centres, identified that diarrhoea was more likely to occur when the same people who change nappies also prepare or serve food. Education of staff in regard to modes of transmission of pathogens, indications for handwashing and the use of gloves has been demonstrated as being important infection control measures.[12]

The provision of adequate toilet facilities has been highlighted and recommendations made that there should be one toilet per ten children.[13] Inadequate numbers of toilets may result in environmental contamination with enteric organisms.

Adequate facilities are an important factor in the promotion of effective handwashing. The numbers and locations of basins should be taken into consideration during the planning stage of any nursery. Sinks should particularly be located in high risk areas such as nappy changing areas, toilets and food preparation areas.

Laundry equipment should be located away from the kitchen area to reduce the risk of introducing faecal pathogens from soiled clothing.[14]

The disposal of waste which includes nappies is an issue which does cause some controversy. Soiled nappies contain excreta which although usually presenting only a low level of risk should be treated as clinical waste.

Food Hygiene

The hygienic preparation of food, combined with effective cleaning of food preparation areas and equipment, and a high standard of personal hygiene is of major importance in preventing contamination of food and subsequent infection.
Policies and procedures in relation to the preparation, storage and serving of food should be familiar to all staff within the nursery setting and should be strictly adhered to. A dishwasher should be used for washing dishes, and kitchen sinks should not be used for any other purpose but cleaning of kitchen equipment.[14] A separate handwash basin is required.

The Child

Prior to enrolment, the parent should complete a vaccination and health record to help assess the child's immunity to childhood illnesses.

Children should be taught how and when to wash their hands properly, and handwashing should be supervised. Play must also be observed and children discouraged from putting shared toys in their mouth.

Feeding bottle and teething aids should be disinfected in a cold sterilizing unit until the child is one year old. A hypochlorite solution containing 1% available chlorine diluted to a 1:80 solution should be used, and be changed daily.

A major source of conflict between parents and staff arises over ill children. Parents criticise staff for excluding children believing their child has become ill because of exposure to a disease at the day care facility, whilst staff may be critical of parents who attempt to bring sick children to the centre. Staff and parents feel tensions from a problem which neither group can solve.

One study[15] compared the opinions of day care staff, working mothers and paediatricians regarding the exclusion of sick children. The results showed day care staff to be more conservative than mothers and paediatricians because they believed that:

- exclusion of ill children significantly reduced the number of secondary cases;
- mildly ill children will increase the workload by requiring extra time and attention;
- they feel uncomfortable in monitoring a child for serious changes in health;
- the child will recover more rapidly if resting in bed at home.

All parties in the study agreed that children with an elevated temperature and other specific signs and symptoms such as diarrhoea should be excluded. The age of the child was not considered to be an important factor.

A trend is emerging in part of America to provide day care for ill children. This is being approached in several ways:

- "sick wing" - cohorting children with similar illness together;
- staff from the nursery care for the ill child in its own home;
- day care centres specifically designed to care for ill children.

However, restrictions are necessary in respect of the type of illness that can be cared for within day care settings[5] and very specific policies must be developed and adhered to. At present policies vary widely, and are often unwritten but more commonly unwritten. Any policies related to providing care for sick children, or their exclusion, should be developed prior to the actual occurrence.

The Staff

All staff should have a recognised certificate in childcare, or be working to achieve this. Ideally staff should work in a designated area with a specific group of children. The decline of childhood antibodies, non-contact with a disease, or an incomplete vaccination programme are all factors which make an adult more susceptible to childhood infectious diseases. An ill adult may also pose a communicable disease risk to the child.

Guidelines for restricting the work practices of the employee with a communicable disease should exist and be discussed with staff prior to employment.

Education and Policies

A study of infection control practice in 12 day care centres, showed that 70% of day care employers did not provide their staff with inservice education related to infection control.[16]

The employees did not understand how diseases were transmitted, nor did they have guidelines for managing a child with an infectious disease. The authors felt that the level of education did not correlate with the knowledge needed to prevent, recognize, control or report the infectious diseases common to day care centres. They recommended that programmes be designed to teach staff members the necessary techniques to control infection. Other work has shown that centres with formal handwashing procedures had a lower incidence of contaminated hands and fomites than those without a formal programme.[8] Hand washing was not being performed consistently between all child contacts and there was a 16% frequency of faecal coliforms on the hands of staff members. It was recommended that a policy for handwashing at set times was drawn up for children and staff.

Osterholm[3] stated that any training must include staff, parents and children to improve the quality of practice. Health education for these groups should improve the overall health of the children. Gillis and colleagues[17] demonstrated that a specific education programme resulted in improvements in staff knowledge regarding common illnesses and infection control practices. Video tapes and resource books were used to outline the providers' responsibilities.

All day care centres should have written infection control policies and procedures.

They should be:
- concise, yet specific, for example cleaning policies should indicate the cleaning agent and the frequency of cleaning;
- written so parents and staff can understand them;
- given to parents to read prior to a child's enrolment.

It is essential that infection control becomes an integral part of providing care within the day care setting. A comprehensive education programme and compliance with policies and procedures will result in a high standard of infection control practice.

REFERENCES
1. Baker T P H. Infection control for the day care facility. ASEPSIS - The Infection Control Forum. 1987; 9(1): 7-11.
2. Sunday Times 1989, 24 September.
3. Osterholm M T. Infection control for the day care facility. ASEPSIS - The Infection Control Forum. 1987; 9(1): 2-5.
4. Feeg V D. Let's face it about day care. Paediat Nurs 1987; 13(3): 148, 154.
5. Russell B. Infection control for the day care facility. ASEPSIS - The Infection Control Forum 1987; 9(1): 11-13.
6. Berg R. Day care for children in the APIC curriculum for infection control practice. Iowa: Kendall/Hunt 1988: 1310-24.
7. Ayliffe G A J, Collins B J, Taylor L J. Hospital acquired infection - principles and prevention. 2nd ed. London: Wright, 1990.
8. Holoday B, Pantell R H, Lewis C C, Gillis C L. Patterns of faecal coliform contamination in day care centres. Public Health Nursing 1990; 7(4): 224-7.
9. Chorba T L, Merriwether R A, Jenkins B R, Gunn R A, MacCormack J N. Control of non-food borne outbreak of Salmonellosis: day care in isolation. Am J Public Health 1987; 77(8): 979-81.
10. Wilson J, Breedon. Universal Precautions. Nursing Times 1990; 86(37): 67-70.
11. Bonner A F, Dale R. Giardia lamblia day care diarrhoea. Am J Nurs 1986; 86(7): 818-20..
12. Butz A M, Larson E, Fosarelli P, Yolken R. Occurrence of infectious symptoms in children in day care homes. Am J Infect Control 1990; 118(6): 347-530.
13. The Childrens Act (1986). Consultation Paper Number 2. Policy and standards of day care and educational services (Guidance). London: DOH, 1990.
14. Smith D P. Common day care diseases: patterns and prevention. Paediat Nurs 1986; 12(3): 175-9.
15. Landis S E, Earp J A L, Sharp M. Day care center exclusion of sick children: comparison of opinion of day care staff, working mothers and pediatricians. Pediatrics 1988; 81(5): 662-6.
16. Lopez J, Diliberto J, McGukin M. Infection control in day care centers: present and future needs. Am J Infect Control 1988; 16(1): 26-9.
17. Gillis G L, Holoday B, Lewis C C, Pantell R H. A health education programme for day care centers. Am J Maternity Child Nursing 1989; 14(4): 266-8.

Professor C. Wastell

Infection Control and Day Surgery

Introduction

In 1940 a typical patient for inguinal hernia repair was admitted to the surgical ward two days pre-operatively for preparation. Post-operatively there followed 21 days of watchful expectancy and strict bed-rest. The aim was to ensure that any complications, including wound infections, were treated promptly and efficiently before discharge.

Typical older style ward

A generation later the situation is very difficult; many hernia operations are performed on a 'Same Day Surgery' basis and the majority of patients spend less than three days in hospital. In 1994 it is estimated that 25-30% of all elective surgical procedures will be performed on a day surgery basis. The patient's post-operative care is managed by a nominated carer, a friend or relative, who escorts the patient from hospital to home, and who is then responsible for 24 hour care until the patient recovers. This clearly has enormous implications for the community health team.

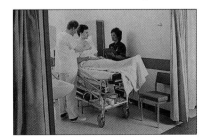

A modern day surgery unit.
Reception Area (left) and Ward Area (right)

Background

Early ambulation was first advocated by Emil Reis of Chicago in 1899[1] but his ideas were not widely accepted until the late 1950s. Farquarson of Edinburgh Royal Infirmary was one of the first to report a large series of day surgery hernia repairs in 1955.[2] These patients were operated on under local anaesthetic and sent home by ambulance before the anaesthetic wore off, the author noted that not all patients arrived home in complete comfort!

The main moves towards more day surgery are both patient driven and economic; patients are less exposed to hospital routine and health service managers see it as a means of reducing expenditure. By keeping the ward open only during normal working hours, costs for nursing staff, heating, lighting are cut; yet, at the same time, an increased number of patients are treated. Many surgeons have expressed the need for caution when expanding day surgery. Their rationale is that limited facilities are available for managing post-operative pain and post-operative complications in day surgery.

Nevertheless there are undoubted benefits from day surgery. It is popular with patients as it allows surgery to be performed with minimal disruption of working and domestic life. It also means that patients are not dependent on vacant beds in the 'main' hospital so a cancellation of their operation is unlikely. From a staffing perspective day units can attract experienced nursing staff whose other commitments prevent them from working shifts or night duties on normal wards.

Definitions

A surgical day case is a patient who is admitted for investigation or treatment on a planned non-resident basis but who still requires facilities for recovery post-operatively. In some units the definition is expanded to include patients who have minor surgical procedures under local anaesthetic. A patient's suitability for day case surgery is assessed in the out-patient clinic by a Consultant or Higher Surgical Trainee and further assessed in the routine booking clinic. When selecting patients for day surgery there are several important criteria. Those at the extremes of age (younger than one year or older than 70 years) are usually excluded unless local or regional anaesthetics are employed. However the biological, rather than chronological age, is more important in the elderly and this must be determined by the clinician during assessment. A carer must be available to accompany the patient to and from the unit and be able to provide 24 hour support. The patient or carer must have access to a telephone for emergencies and the patient's home should be within a journey time of one hour from the hospital by car. For general anaesthetic cases patients should be American Society of Anesthesiologists Grade I (normal) or ASA II (minor systemic disease which is well controlled with treatment and does not interfere with normal activities). Patients who are grossly obese (Body Mass Index greater than 30) should be excluded.

The selection process has an important impact on the frequency of post-operative infections. Patients known to be at a higher risk of infection, such as insulin dependent diabetics, the elderly, and the obese should normally be excluded. The importance of this type of selection was confirmed by Zoutman in 1990[3] who found an overall infection rate as low as 5.0% in a series of 635 patients undergoing day surgery.

To maintain the highest standards, day surgery should be carried out by experienced, fully trained surgeons and anaesthetists operating well within their own range of ability in accordance with recommendations by the Royal College of Surgeons (RCS).[4] Trainee surgeons should only operate in the day unit under the close personal supervision of consultant staff. Some technical points include analgesia and suturing; including the use of local nerve blocks to provide better initial analgesia while other analgesics take effect. Subcuticular sutures, preferably absorbable (RCS guidelines) under a transparent dressing, avoids the necessity for nursing staff to remove sutures and also allows easy inspection of the wound. Usually these dressings can be left in place until the skin has healed and they do not inhibit normal washing by the patient.

The ideal day surgery unit is a self contained facility with its own admission suite, wards, theatre and recovery area. This permits an individual unit policy for all procedures, including infection control. The operating theatre should be of the same standard as a normal main operating theatre with adequate lighting, ventilation, scrub-up and waste disposal systems. The more modern day units provide each patient with his/her own bed which doubles as a trolley and an operating table.

Unfortunately financial constraints mean that this ideal is not possible in many hospitals. Often a day case ward (such as a closed down general ward) or allocated beds on a general surgical ward are used. The operations in these hospitals are usually performed in main theatres either as dedicated day surgery lists or as part of normal operating lists. Obviously there are drawbacks with these methods. Day patients are at risk of being cancelled, either by emergency cases or because lists overrun their allocated time in operating theatres. If the allocated day surgery beds are not protected from occupation by emergency admissions several days of day surgery lists may have to be cancelled.

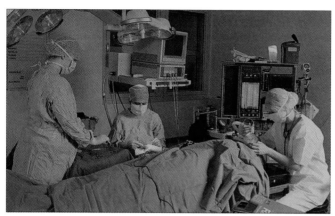

Photograph of modern day unit operating theatre

Infection Control

Blood and body fluids may contain bacterial or viral pathogens which present a hazard to other patients or members of staff. It is usually impossible to tell which patients are carrying these pathogens. As part of good practice theatre staff should follow satisfactory universal precautions in the day unit. From an infection control perspective identification and isolation of sources of infection is more difficult in a mixed unit. Day surgery units eliminate post-operative infection of wounds on the ward, although this has been shown to be rare; most infections are introduced into a wound once the skin has been incised. The majority of infections come from the patient's own microbial skin flora, the remainder are acquired from operating room staff or from circulating organisms from the air in theatre. Both of these factors can be minimised by using adequate patient skin preparation (with alcoholic betadine or chlorhexidine) and by staff using bacteria-impermeable clothing. The peak bacterial count in an operating theatre is at the end of the procedure when staff are preparing for the next case by taking instruments and drapes away.[5] This can be reduced by good staff discipline, but during a busy day surgery list it can sometimes be difficult to restrict the number of staff circulating, opening and closing doors to the theatre.

Types of Operation

The case mix in a day unit is larger than in a general unit. Varying from gynaecologists carrying out terminations, urologists performing vasectomies and flexible cystoscopies as well as orthopaedic surgeons performing arthroscopies and general surgeons repairing hernias and removing varicose veins. To ensure that time is used efficiently and cross contamination is avoided between specialties each day surgery session should ideally be used by a single team or firm of surgeons with a break for theatre cleaning and for the ventilation system to have completed at least one air change.

It is traditional to classify operations by infection risk according to the NAS/NRC system.[6]

- Clean - non-traumatic procedure with no break in surgical technique. The respiratory, gastro-intestinal and genito-urinary tracts are not entered (e.g. inguinal hernia repair).
- Clean-contaminated - respiratory, gastro-intestinal or urinary tract (not infected) entered, but without significant spillage (e.g. laparoscopic cholecystectomy).
- Contaminated - procedure in which spillage from a body cavity occurs but no pus is encountered.
- Dirty/infected - major break in technique during the operation, a traumatic wound or gross spillage from an infected body cavity (e.g. pilonidal sinus, or abscess).

Clearly the infection rate should be lowest in the first category and highest in the last category. The majority of procedures performed in the day unit are clean or clean-contaminated and as a consequence wound infection rates have been found to be significantly lower in day surgery,[3] although there are few reports of purely day surgery.

The move to independence is emphasised by the fact that the modern day surgery unit now has its own autoclave, for sterilising instruments, and glutaraldehyde cleaning systems, for cleaning endoscopic equipment following Control of Substances Hazardous to Health (COSHH) guidelines.[7] These are subject to the usual checks on effectiveness at regular intervals and avoids a dependence on a remote theatre sterile supplies unit. Day units are increasingly using disposable drapes not just for 'High Risk' and infected case but for clean, elective procedures. The extra cost is outweighted by eliminating the requirement for a linen room and is consistent with universal precautions.

Post-discharge Monitoring

With same day discharge, patient surveillance is no longer carried out by ward nursing staff. Immediately after the operation the patient returns to the recovery area. The operation site is inspected and the general state of the patient is assessed by the operator and anaesthetist prior to discharge. Occasionally admission to hospital may be necessary if recovery is slower than expected or if the operative procedure was unexpectedly complicated. If patient selection is appropriate this should only be required in less than 1% of cases.[8]

Following discharge prompt detection and treatment of complications depends upon the patient or carer and the community nurse. Good patient education is essential and this is accomplished by explanation from day unit staff together with simple, clearly written, information booklets. These should advise about the normal recovery process and describe situations which require further action, such as telephoning the unit or contacting the patient's own general practitioner.

Good communication between the day unit and the primary care team is essential. Many day surgery units employ their own domiciliary nursing staff, but if not the unit should inform the community nurse that a patient is about to be discharged and will require a post-operative visit. A discharge letter must be provided by the operating surgeon informing the general practitioner of the type of procedure and the expected post-operative course. The nursing staff should supply a letter to be given to the community nurse at the first home visit. These initial letters and communication are vital if adequate back up is to be provided in the community for day surgery patients.

The majority of patients should be assessed by the community nurse within 48 hours of discharge as part of routine surveillance. Any complications detected can be referred to the general practitioner or to the surgical team responsible for that patient.

Some wound infections after hospital discharge are inevitable. Previous studies of post discharge infections in all patients, not just day surgery, have varied between 3.8% and 28% [9, 10, 11] depending upon the method of assessment used. The lowest reported rates were in purely clinic based studies where the assessment was by the operating surgeon. The highest rates were in studies where patients were given a questionnaire and reassessed by an independent observer. One study from Texas by Weigel,[12] followed 16,453 patients for 30 days after operation. The in-hospital infection rate was 5.8% but a further 516 patients (35% of those with infection) developed an infection at home to give a true rate of 8.9%. Moreover they found that delayed manifestations of infection were more likely in clean operations, shorter operations, obese patients and non-alcoholic patients, and of great importance was the fact that many infections did not become obvious until twenty-one days post operation.

In the United States, where day surgery is extremely popular, concern has been raised about the post-discharge infection rates. A recent review in the American Journal of Infection Control[13] commented that 20% to 70% of postoperative surgical site infections did not become apparent until after discharge from further out-patient surveillance. The authors called for new national guidelines for a quality infection control programme, as neither the Centers for Disease Control nor the Joint Commission for the Accreditation of Healthcare Organisations currently have such guidelines.

There has only been one published study of wound infections after discharge in this country so far by Law and colleagues.[14] They carried out a prospective study of 1,242 patients including 156 day cases. From an overall infection rate of 6.7%, 41% were diagnosed in hospital and 59% in the community.

Conclusions

If day surgery expands to the predicted target of 50% of all elective cases then many patients at higher risk of infection will have more complex procedures in the day unit. Indeed some surgeons already perform thyroidectomies,[15, 16] superficial parotidectomies,[17, 18] and laparoscopic cholecystectomies[19] on day patients. The only way that this can be achieved safely and effectively is with senior surgical, anaesthetic and nursing staff together with a well informed, well motivated patient and good community support.

REFERENCES
1. Reis E. Some radical changes in the after-treatment of celotomy cases. JAMA 1899; 33: 454-6.
2. Farquharson E L. Early ambulation with special reference to herniorrhaphy as an outpatient procedure. Lancet 1955; 2: 517-9.
3. Zoutnun D, Pearce P, McKenzie M, Taylor G. Surgical wound infections occurring in day surgery patients. Am J Infect Control 1990; 18(4): 277-82.
4. Royal College of Surgeons of England. Commission on Provision of Surgical Services: report of the working party of the guidelines for day case surgery. London: RCS, 1992.
5. Ayliffe G A J. Role of the environment of the operating suite in surgical wound infection. Rev Infect Dis 1991; 13(Suppl 10): S800-04.
6. National Research Council. Post-operative wound infections. The influence of ultraviolet irradiation of the operating room and of various other factors. Ann Surg 1964; 160:(Suppl 2, Ch4): 32-81.
7. Health and Safety Commission. Control of substances hazardous to health (general acop) and control of carcinogenic substances. (Carcinogens Acop):COSHH Regulations 1988; 4th ed. London: HMSO, 1993.
8. Johnson C D, Jarrett P E. Admission to hospital after day case surgery. Ann R Coll Surg Engl 1990; 72: 225-8.
9. Polk B F, Shapiro M, Goldstein P, Tager I B, Goren-White B, Schoenbaum S C Randomised clinical trial of perioperative Cefazolin in preventing infection after hysterectomy. Lancet 1980; 1: 437-40.
10. Burns S J, Dippe S E. Postoperative wound infections detected during hospitalisation and after discharge in a community hospital. Am J Infect Control 1982; 10: 60-5.
11. Donovan I A, Ellis D, Gatehouse D, et al. One dose antibiotic prophylaxis against wound infection after appendicectomy: a randomised trial of Clindamycin, Cefazolin sodium and A placebo. Br J Surg 1979; 66: 193-6.
12. Weigelt J A, Dryer D, Haley R W. The necessity and efficiency of wound surveillance after discharge. Arch Surg 1992; 127(1): 77-82.
13. Holtz T H, Wenzel R P. Postdischarge surveillance for nosocomial wound infection: a brief review and commentary. Am J Infect Control 1992; 20(4): 206-13.
14. Law D J, Mishriki S F, Jeffery P J. The importance of surveillance after discharge from hospital in the diagnosis of postoperative wound infection. Ann R Coll Surg Engl 1990; 72(3): 207-9.
15. Lo Gerfo P, Gates R, Gazetas P. Out-patient and short stay thyroid surgery Head Neck 1991; 13(2): 97-101.
16. Mishra S K, Sharma A K, Thakur S. Out patient and short stay thyroid surgery. Head & Neck 1992; 14(3): 247-8.
17. Steckler R M. Out-patient parotidectomy. Am J Surg 1991; 162(4): 303-5.
18. Helmus C, Grin M, Westfall R. Same-day-stay head and neck surgery. Laryngoscope 1992; 102: 1331-4.
19. Arregui M E, Davis C J, Arkush ., Nagan R F. In selected patients out-patient laparoscopic cholecystectomy is safe and significantly reduces hospitalization charges. Surg Laparosc Endosc 1991; 1(4): 240-5.

Mrs Debra Khan

Chapter 9

Infection Control and the Ambulance Service

The ambulance service in England and Wales began in 1948 with the introduction of the National Health Service Act (1946).[1] This act gave local authorities the responsibility of ensuring a free transport system for patients to and from treatment centres. In 1974 this responsibility was transferred to the NHS and provisions were provided by Regional and District Health Authorities. As with all health care settings many ambulance services have now become self-governing trusts.

The role of the ambulance service is to provide an appropriate form of transport for the public who are unable, for medical reasons, to make their own way to hospital, and the necessary first aid on site and en route to the hospital.

The work load falls into two main categories:
- emergency work involving 999 calls, urgent calls and transfers of critically ill patients between hospitals. This accounts for approximately 20% of the work load;[2]
- non-emergency transportation, e.g. patient admissions, discharges, transfers between hospital and transport to outpatients and clinics.

Each ambulance crew consists of a driver and an attendant. The attendant can either be trained as a technician or as a paramedic. The technician is trained in basic first aid and life support. The paramedic receives a more extensive training in saving lives and reducing morbidity and mortality.

Infection Control Risks Related to the Ambulance Service

Since the development of AIDS more research has been focused on infection control and protection of health care workers. There has been very little work directed at ambulance personnel and most advice given has been adapted from research related to other health care settings.[3] Infection risks to patients are considered to be low due to the inanimate environment and the short period spent within the ambulance.[4] However, when developing an infection control strategy the unpredictable situation and uncontrolled conditions that ambulance personnel work within must be taken into account.

The ambulance personnel are the 'front line' of the health service and are usually the first health care professionals to attend a sick patient. This may be a person unconscious due to unknown cause or a patient with severe traumatic injuries from a road traffic accident. At this early stage any infection a patient may be suffering from is generally unknown. Advice given to ambulance control on receipt of a call usually contains minimal information and the patient may not be able or willing to pass on any relevant information. There is often exposure to blood and body fluids such as diarrhoea and vomit, and the advances in paramedic training have now increased pre-hospital care to involve intubation and insertion of vascular devices.[6] Infectious disease likely to be encountered by ambulance staff include tuberculosis, meningitis, gastrointestinal illnesses such as dysentery, and hepatitis B and HIV/AIDS.

Staff and Patient Protection

Although space is limited on board an ambulance all emergency ambulances should carry the following equipment in order to protect staff and patients from potential cross infection:
- alcohol hand rub;
- disposable latex gloves;
- disposable aprons;
- eye protection/visor;
- heavy-duty gloves;
- yellow clinical waste bags;
- sharps box;
- portable sharps box for paramedic use;
- white laundry bags;
- red laundry bags;
- sodium hypochlorite tablets;
- sodium hypochlorite granules;
- disposable clothes for cleaning;
- alcohol wipes suitable for cleaning equipment;
- adequate supply of the following disposables: oxygen masks, tubing, nebulisers, vomit bowels, suction tubing and catheter.

It is important that ambulance personnel have a good service from occupational health departments. This service should include the checking of immunity to poliomyelitis, tetanus, tuberculosis and rubella, and immunisation offered as necessary. Due to their potential contact with blood and body fluids all personnel should be offered hepatitis B vaccine with follow-up to check antibody levels and administration of booster doses as required. Good communications and clearly defined policies in connection with inoculation injuries are vital in order for ambulance personnel to be advised and counselled as promptly as possible. Reassurance may be necessary from occupational health if contact with infections such as tuberculosis, HIV or meningitis has occurred, particularly if a patient has died. Prophylactic antibiotics may be necessary in a case of meningitis if mouth-to-mouth resuscitation was attempted.[7] However this is only undertaken following advice from the Department of Public Health Medicine.

Handwashing is considered the most important procedure that can prevent cross infection and protect health care workers.[8] Facilities are not available on the ambulance so it is therefore important that handwashing is undertaken after dispatch of patients to health care settings or their homes. An alcohol hand rub may be used as an alternative if facilities are unsuitable or unavailable particularly prior to performing an invasive procedure on site.[4]

Protective clothing should always be available on board the ambulance. Recent publications from the Health and Safety Commission on Personnel Protective Equipment at Work[9] has further emphasised the responsibility of both employers to provide, and employees to wear, appropriate protective clothing during the course of their work.

Gloves should be worn by personnel who have contact with, or who are likely to have contact with, blood or body fluids. Gloves should be non-sterile latex as these provide a better fit, are stronger and resist tearing more readily than plastic gloves.[10] All gloves should be disposed of after the patient has been dispatched and prior to cleaning or handling equipment. If there is a risk of laceration occurring to hands at the site of an accident stronger general purpose gloves may be worn over the disposable ones.

Eye protection should be worn if there is likely to be body fluid spiashes into the eyes. This may also be required whilst patients are being cut free from car wreckage. Protective, waterproof overalls are not required for protection against infectious diseases but may have some value against infestations. If there is a risk of uniforms becoming contaminated with body fluids a plastic apron should be worn. Facilities should be made available for staff to change grossly contaminated uniforms and have showers as necessary.

Decontamination of the Ambulance Vehicle and Equipment

Routine cleaning of vehicles usually takes place during the quieter periods mainly on Sundays. During these times a reduced number of ambulance crews are on duty thus releasing several ambulances. However, reduced levels of staff have made cleaning schedules difficult to keep to and rotational cleaning of vehicles is generally undertaken.[11]

When ambulances become contaminated cleaning of surfaces and equipment must take place after dispatch of the patient to the accident and emergency department or other settings prior to the next call of duty. Effective, manageable and realistic policies need to be in place to achieve this within a short period of time. This is necessary due to pressure put on the ambulance personnel to activate an ambulance and arrive at the scene within a set time. These response rates are closely monitored as part of the 'Orcon standards' of performance.[12]

Decontamination should be carried out at the accident and emergency department or relevant health care setting. Vehicles should have all movable equipment removed, and contaminated surfaces and floors should be cleaned with a sodium hypochlorite solution 10,000 parts per million. Disposable clothes and mops should be used for widespread spillage and granules for a smaller, contained, spillage. The use of formaldehyde vapour for stoving vehicles is no longer required to decontaminate the ambulance.[4] Hosing down the inside of vehicles using a water spray should be avoided as this can cause splashing and create aerosols which can potentially contaminate staff. All surfaces should be allowed to dry thoroughly before the ambulance is put back into use. Any single-use medical equipment should be disposed of at the hospital and replaced. It is important that an adequate supply of single-use equipment is always available and replenished when used to avoid the need for reuse. Reusable equipment must remain out of service until it is cleaned, disinfected and dried. For recommended methods of decontamination see Table 1.

Table 1

Decontamination of medical equipment

Airways (all types)	Wash with warm soapy water. Dry thoroughly. Store dry in a dust proof cover.
Bedpans/Urinals	Use disposable. Dispose of at hospital.
Body bags	Use heavy duty type only. Disposable.
Defibrillator paddles	After patient use wash with warm soapy water and dry thoroughly. If visibly contaminated, wipe with 70% alcohol wipe and allow to dry.
Drinking cups	Disposable.
Endotracheal tubes Catheter mounts	Store in dust proof bags. Disposable once used.
Forceps, Magills, Spencer Wells	After use wash with warm soapy water and dry thoroughly. Wipe with 70% alcohol wipe.
Intravenous cannulae giving sets Dressing	Keep sterile until required for use. Use sterile covering to secure cannulae
Laryngoscope blade	Disposable Reusable. Wash with warm soapy water. Unscrew light bulb to ensure washed well. Wipe with 70% alcohol wipe. Allow to dry.
Nebulisers Masks Tubing	Single patient use only. May go with the patient once admitted to hospital. Otherwise disposable.
Oxygen masks Tubing	Single patient use only. May go with the patient once admitted to hospital. Otherwise disposable.
Pulse oximeter	Wash with warm soapy water. If visibly contaminated wipe with 70% alcohol wipe.

Table 1 continued

Splints, Collars	Wash with warm soapy water. If visibly contaminated wipe with 70% alcohol wipe.
Stretcher	Wash with warm soapy water. If visibly contaminated, with alcohol wipe.
Suction:	
Catheter	Single use only. Dispose between patient use. Do not connect to tubing when not in use.
Tubing	Single use, disposable.
Bottle	Clean with warm soapy water and dry thoroughly. Store dry.
Thermometer rectal/oral	Wash with warm soapy water. Wipe with 70% alcohol wipe.
Thermos flask	Wash flask daily. Change water daily.
Vomit Bowls	Single use only. dispose of at hospital or base.

Clinical Waste and Sharps Safety

Clinical waste and sharps generated by ambulance staff have presented problems.[11] Guidelines for the ambulance service have now been included in the Health Service Advisory Committee guidance on Safe Disposal of Clinical Waste.[13] All vehicles used for routine and emergency transport should carry yellow plastic bags for clinical waste disposal. These bags should be sealed, labelled and disposed of with dispatch of the patient, usually at the hospital. Local arrangements with hospitals need to be agreed to ensure this process works effectively. If disposed of at the ambulance base, waste should be stored in a locked designated area until collection and disposal by incineration in accordance with current legislation. A suitably sized sharps box should be available on each ambulance. This should conform with the British Standard BS7320.[14] The sharps box should be closed and stored in a secure place when not in use so that spillage of contents does not occur. A smaller, portable sharps box should be available for use by paramedics attending patients away from the ambulance. It should be securely placed in the paramedics holdall. These boxes should be disposed of when three-quarters full or periodically if used infrequently. All ambulance staff required to handle clinical waste and sharps should be trained in its safe handling and disposal and should know what action to take in the case of a spillage. This training should include a basic minimum for all staff with more information related to the use of sharps for paramedics.

Laundry

All linen used on the ambulance should be changed daily. If it becomes contaminated or is used by a known infected patient it must be changed as soon as is practicable. Laundry bags for linen disposal should be available on the ambulance and colour coded according to local policy.

Clinical Procedures

Over recent years there has been an increase in the pre-hospital care given by ambulance men known as paramedics. these personnel are specifically trained in conjunction with the Paramedic Training Manual[6] to perform:
- electrocardiograph monitoring defibrillation;
- intubation;
- intravenous cannulae insertion and infusions of fluids and drugs.

The training programme is extensive with practical experience gained in the accident and emergency department and by working closely with an anaesthetist. Each ambulance department participates in a national paramedic audit scheme.[6] This audit monitors performance in the use of extended skills: how often a procedure has been used; whether it was relevant and whether it was successful. Individual retraining and updating of staff is dependent on these results.

Each paramedic is issued with a holdall that he is specifically responsible for. This holdall contains all the necessary equipment to perform the procedures described above. The holdall is portable and can be taken with the paramedic to wherever the patient requires treatment. To prevent environmental soiling and equipment becoming wet the holdall should be waterproof and easily cleaned. All sterile equipment must remain sealed in its packing until required for use, e.g. intravenous cannulae. Equipment such as airways and suction machines should be protected from soiling by placing in dust proof packages.

The paramedic receives training in the insertion of intravenous cannulae and the administration of fluids and drugs with a priority to save lives. Normal preparations and aseptic techniques should be applied, if time allows, but this is rarely possible in emergencies. However everything should be done as cleanly and aseptically as possible. This can be achieved by having equipment readily available. A sterile dressing must be placed over the cannula to keep it secure whilst the patient is being transferred. The use of tape to secure cannulae should be avoided as this is often contaminated.[15] Once a patient is stable in hospital these initial cannulae should be replaced under more ideal conditions.

Mouth-to-mouth resuscitation using expired air poses minimal risk to ambulance personnel.[5] Ambulance personnel have advanced training in airway maintenance and devices such as Brookes airway and resusiade are used; both of these devices prevent contact with a patient and his secretions. Although mouth-to-mouth resuscitation whilst on duty is not encouraged it is left to the discretion of the individual.

Infectious Diseases

When ambulance control receive a call basic information is requested. This is coded so ambulance personnel are fully informed and able to meet the needs of patients whilst being transported. Information should include any infection suspected. All health care personnel requesting an ambulance have a moral and ethical obligation to give accurate information to the crews so that they can follow advice and guidelines as necessary. This will also ensure that information is passed on to hospitals and other health settings accepting the patient, and will reduce any unnecessary anxieties to ambulance personnel who may later hear that the patient is in isolation or may have died from an infection.

The Basic Training Manual[2] for ambulance staff classifies infectious diseases into three categories according to the action necessary during ambulance transport:

Category One	No precautions necessary	e.g. malaria
Category Two	Simple precautions	e.g. tuberculosis, hepatitis B
Category Three	Special precautions	e.g. Lassa fever

These three categories have been clearly defined in order to accurately inform staff of the infection risks, if any, and of any precautions that they need to take. Category One refers to infections such as malaria and glandular fever where there is no risk to staff. Apart from a universal approach to contact with body fluids no further precautions are necessary.

Category Two includes infection where there is an identified small risk to personnel and potential contamination of the environment is possible. This is mainly related to body fluid spillage and advice about decontamination, linen disposal and follow up advice for staff is required. (See Table 2: Diseases and Procedures).

Category Three infections are specifically related to viral haemorrhagic fevers such as Lassa fever and Marburg fever. When one of these diseases is confirmed or suspected specific guidelines issued by the Department of Health[16] are followed. More specific advice about staff protection and any other precautions are usually given directly to ambulance personnel from the accepting hospital. In previous years a designated ambulance and crew has been available in each Regional Health Authority for the transport of Category Three infections. These crews were required to wear protective clothing such as waterproof overalls, rubber boots and visors. Specific precautions at this level are now no longer undertaken and if required an emergency ambulance is adapted to transport these patients. This usually involved removing extraneous items and only carrying the minimal amount of equipment required. The remaining equipment should be protected with plastic coverings and the windows through to the driver's area sealed.

More recently concerns have been raised in connection with methicillin resistant *Staphylococcus aureus* (MRSA) and transfer of infected or colonised patients. This is confusing for ambulance personnel due to different policies in relation to isolation and staff screening. Consequently advice about decontamination of equipment and the environment can differ. Most MRSA infections can be safely transported in the ambulance, provided all wounds are covered and any body fluid spillage is cleaned up promptly. After dispatch of patient used linen should be disposed in accordance with local policy and the immediate area wiped with an alcohol wipe.

Due to the unpredictable situation and rapid response of the ambulance crew information in relation to infection control procedures needs to be easily assessable. The operational procedure manual cannot always be stored in the ambulance due to limited space.

An adapted version of Tables 1 and 2 on laminated card can be a useful reference guide for staff and stored easily within the drivers cabin.

Education and Training

Education of ambulance personnel in infection control is undertaken during the initial Basic Training Course in conjunction with the Basic Training Manual.[2] Although more extensive training is undertaken for paramedics there is no further set training in infection control and this is usually dealt with during the hospital experience.

Updates are usually undertaken by infection control teams and occupational health nurses on an *ad hoc* basis. It is important that education is aimed at increasing awareness of standards of hygiene, reiteration of basic training principles and precautions necessary to maintain safe practice. However to ensure this training is effective an understanding of the circumstances of the daily work of ambulance staff is required.[5] All ambulance personnel need to be aware of the nature of infections, the route of spread and how this relates to their day to day work and the procedures that they undertake.

Table II
Diseases and Procedures
(Adapted from the West Midlands Ambulance Service Quality Management System)

DISEASE	INFECTIOUS RISK	PRECAUTIONS	FOLLOW-UP
CATEGORY ONE			
Malaria, Glandular fever	None	None necessary	None
CATEGORY TWO			
Food Poisoning e.g. Dysentery, Cholera, Salmonella	Minimal if contact with faeces and vomit	Wear gloves contact with body fluids Dispose of contaminated linen as infected	Contact occupational health if grossly contaminated
Pulmonary Tuberculosis	Minimal due to immunisation Respiratory secretions	No specific precautions	Contact occupational health
AIDS	Only if exposed to blood or body fluids	Wear gloves if contact with body fluids Dispose of contaminated linen as infected Clean up spillages promptly with sanichlor 10,000 parts per million Wear gloves and aprons	Contact occupational health if contamination occurs
Hepatitis B	Only if exposed to blood or body fluids	Wear gloves if contact with body fluids Dispose of contaminated linen as infected Clean up spillages promptly with sanichlor 10,000 parts per million Wear gloves and apron	Contact occupational health if contamination occurs
Meningococcal Meningitis	Only if mouth to mouth resuscitation attempted	Use protective resuscitation equipment	Contact occupational health if mouth to mouth resuscitation occurred
MRSA (Methicillin Resistant *Staphylococcus aureus*)	No risk to personnel May be passed on to other patients	Wear gloves and aprons for contact with body fluids Wash hands thoroughly after patient dispatch Wipe patient area with alcohol wipe. Dispose of linen as infected	
CATEGORY THREE			
	High risk Specific guidelines required		
Infestations	Minimal	Wear gloves and aprons for patient contact Dispose of linen as infected	

REFERENCES
1. Ministry of Health. The National Health Service Act 1946. London: HMSO, 1946.
2. National Health Service Training Department. Ambulance service basic training manual. London: NHS, 1988.
3. ICNA Wessex Groups, 1991 (unpublished).
4. Ayliffe G A J, Lowbury E J, Geddes A M, Williams J D.Control of hospital infection; a practical handbook. 3rd ed. London: Chapman & Hall Medical, 1992.
5. D'Auria D. AIDS & ambulance staff: are your men safe? Ambulance Management International 1987: 19-21.
6. National Health Service Training Directorate. Ambulance service paramedic training London: NHS, 1991.
7. PHLS Meningococcal Infections Working Party. The epidemiology and control of Meningococcal Disease. PHLS Commun Dis Rep 1989; P+ 8 3-6.
8. Reybrouck G. Handwashing and hand disinfection. J Hosp Infect 1986; 8(1): 5-23.
9. Health and Safety executive. Personnel protective equipment at work. Guidance on regulations. London: HMSO, 1992.
10. Klein R C, Party E, Gershey E L. Virus penetration of examination gloves. Biotechniques 1990; 9(2): 196-9.
11. Skovgaard P. (1989) Ambulance watch. J Infection Control Nursing /Nursing Times 1989; 85(49): 63-7.
12. Operational Research in Health. Review of ambulance service standards: emergency and urgent targets. Final report. London: HMSO, 1990.
13. Health Service Advisory Committee. Safe disposal of clinical waste. London: HMSO, 1992.
14. British Standards Institute. BS7320; Specification for sharps containers. London: BSI, 1990.
15. Oldman P. A sticky situation? Microbiological study of adhesive tape used to secure IV cannulae. Prof Nurse 1991; 6(5): 265-6, 268-9.
16. DHSS. Memorandum on the control of viral haemorrhagic fevers. London: HMSO, 1986.

Dr Richard T. Mayon-White

Chapter 10

Public Health

Public Health Medicine is the science and art of preventing disease, prolonging life and promoting health by the organised efforts of society.[1] The arrangements for providing these functions are so varied that most people are confused by them. This variety of arrangements arises from the wide range of contributors to the public's health amongst which are good housing, safe transport, pure water, equitable health care, adequate food, sewage and waste disposal, employment, education. In addition, solutions to public health problems come from different levels and systems of government; for example, the management of an outbreak requires local action; solutions, such as taxation or legislation to deter harmful practices, require national action; and problems such as the trade in contaminated products require international cooperation for resolution. This chapter aims to explain one small part of this complicated picture, namely the public health aspects of infection control in Great Britain.

In Great Britain, the public health functions of the National Health Service are based on district health authorities or commissions who employ directors of public health and their staff. These departments of public health have a number of functions which are relevant to infection control in the community. The most important being the control of communicable diseases. Links with Family Health Services Authorities and local authorities, contributing to the purchasing functions of health authorities, and assessing the needs of the populations are routine functions of public health doctors, and contribute to the control of infection in the community.

Communicable Disease Control Functions

Responsibility

Every Department of Public Health should have at least one Consultant in Communicable Disease Control (CCDC). This consultant is a senior officer in the Health Authority, carrying the full professional responsibility for the functions described here. Within the Health Authority, the CCDC is accountable to the Director of Public Health, who in turn is accountable to the Chief Executive, and thence to the Health Authority. The CCDC is normally seen by the public and by the Health Authority as the leader for the communicable disease functions of the local health services. This perception is emphasised by the duty of the CCDC to report directly to the Chief Medical Officer at the Department of Health on any major infectious disease incidents in the district.

Communicable Disease Surveillance and Notification

A logical starting point for the control of infection is intelligence on what diseases occur where, when, how often, in whom and why. The basic system for this surveillance is the notification of infectious diseases. Doctors attending a patient with a notifiable infection are legally required to notify the CCDC of the case. This is a law that is ignored as often as it is observed, and is overdue for reform. But it has an important purpose, enabling legally enforceable control measures. As long as under-notification and the errors of some clinical diagnoses are recognised, the notifications are a reasonable guide to the presence of some infections and to the progress in controlling others: a cluster of reports of dysentery or hepatitis A will trigger an investigation into a possible outbreak; the number of measles notifications tells how the immunisation programme is going.

Laboratory reports are another useful source of information on possible outbreaks and other important incidents. The accuracy and the precision of a microbiological diagnosis - confirming and often typing the pathogen - is a good foundation for an epidemiological investigation. Microbiologists generally send copies of laboratory reports relevant to public health to their local CCDC, and telephone about cases of meningitis and early evidence of an outbreak (e.g. a cluster of cases of Legionnaires' disease). The value of the laboratory data in surveillance depends on an adequate flow of specimens to the laboratory from the community. For this, general practitioners and environmental health officers must be sure that the laboratory provides a timely and affordable service, and that the service includes expert advice. The changes in the NHS and the repeated reviews of laboratory services threaten this hitherto satisfactory system.

Whilst notifications and laboratory data are useful, some infections of public health importance need another systems of surveillance. Influenza and chickenpox are not notifiable and are infrequently tested by laboratory specimens. Consultation patterns from sentinel general practices provide consistent information on the incidence of these diseases. The system of sentinel GPs started as a research project in Britain, and has since been copied in other European countries. The system is relatively small and simple. About 100 GPs count every patient that they see with one of a set of infectious diseases, and send in the number seen in each week to a central office. The size and age structure of the recording practices is already known, and weekly rates of infection can therefore be directly calculated. This system gives the fastest and most reliable indication of the usual winter epidemics of influenza, and can detect whether old or young people are more at risk, and has given the only British data on the incidence of scabies, which fluctuates from year to year. A similar sentinel system operates in boarding schools when the schools' medical officers send the information to the national Communicable Diseases Surveillance Centre.

An analysis of the data from death certificates or diagnoses made in hospital can provide information on the more severe community-acquired infections, but this is only useful for reviews and not for immediate control actions.

If an outbreak is suspected, it is often worth setting up a more active surveillance system in an attempt to identify all cases for the duration of the investigation. This would include a letter to local doctors and heads of institutions asking them to report cases and, with the agreement of the laboratory, to send the appropriate specimens.

The press may be asked to inform the public about the illness and to encourage people to report their symptoms to the family doctor. In some instances, everybody at risk is contacted and asked whether they have been ill; this is often done to investigate a food-poisoning outbreak where a group of people attended a party or other function. Whatever method of surveillance is used, and especially with active surveillance, one should have a case-definition, that is a definite criterion as to what makes a person 'a case' in the epidemiological study.

Information and Advice

Surveillance works best when information and advice is fed back to those who report cases. This can be done in several ways. The most informal is a direct exchange of information when cases are reported: staff will be encouraged to report influenza or gastro-enteritis in a nursing home if they are given news of cases elsewhere or advice on infection control measures. Another method is to give a regular bulletin which combines news about topical infection problems, trends in infections locally or nationally, and practical advice. Seminars and visits can offer the same combination. Electronic mail has a place, but it is not as user-friendly as the written or spoken word. The local press are usually grateful for health information and will often turn surveillance data into a readable and interesting story.

Management of Outbreaks

The management of outbreaks is seen by many to be the main communicable disease control function, because it is the most urgent, the most important and the most public. However good outbreak management depends on having three functions working well. The principles of managing outbreaks are the same whether they occur in the hospital or in the community. The first step is to get an accurate diagnosis of the condition supposed to be occurring at more than its expected frequency (the definition of an outbreak) and entails seeing or telephoning those who are ill and the staff looking after them. Once the diagnosis is clear, the next step is to see if there is an outbreak plan that applies. Departments of public health should have plans to handle water-borne outbreaks, food-poisoning, Legionnaires' disease, meningitis, viral haemorrhagic fever, major accidents and chemical incidents. There are likely to be files on dysentery, scabies and influenza which show how problems have been managed in the past. In these plans, there should be lists of people to be contacted, appropriate control measures, resources that are available, and guidance on how the outbreak should be investigated. In difficult or large outbreaks, it is important that an outbreak control team is formed and meets regularly, keeping good records of its decisions and actions. Minor incidents can be managed without outbreak team meetings, but care must be taken to communicate with those involved, not least with the patients and their health care workers. In community outbreaks, communications are likely to need more time and attention than in a hospital. This is not only because of distance, but also because lines of responsibility are more convoluted. The commonest reason for an outbreak being mismanaged is because it is treated as a minor problem when a coordinated outbreak team effort is needed.

Routine Control Measures

There are many ways of controlling infection in the community, and public health departments are partly responsible for purchasing them or providing them. Other agencies which are responsible are local authorities and the provider services. The purpose of this section is to summarise the methods and indicate how they are implemented.

Health education is traditionally a public health function, and one that has proved difficult to fit into the divided purchaser-provider model. The general awareness of infections and information about communicable diseases continues to come from CCDCs and their staff, but education to change behaviour requires skill and time that come best from specialists in education. It is necessary to make alliances between organisations in order to have a convincing and effective health education programme, something that is recognised in the British Government's Health of the Nation strategy.

Vaccination is another health activity associated with public health. In recent years, the administration of vaccines has moved to general practice, usually being done by the increasing number of practice nurses employed by GPs. These vaccines are the routine childhood immunisations, and vaccines for travel abroad. School vaccinations remain one of the functions of the school medical services, but even these are being taken over by general practitioners. Chemoprophylaxis is provided either by hospital staff or GPs on most occasions. CCDCs set the local routine policies, in line with national guidance, and directly provide chemoprophylaxis and vaccines on the occasions when it would be difficult for a GP or hospital to do so.

There are a few times when it is necessary to use formal legal powers to control infection, and many more occasions when the existence of such powers in the background helps to get action taken. The public health medical interest is in the powers related to the person, whilst the environmental health and veterinary officers concentrate on the non-human factors. The legal powers are vested in the local authority, for whom a CCDC is usually a 'proper officer'. Under the Public Health (Control of Disease) Act 1984, a patient with tuberculosis can be compelled to be medically examined or admitted to hospital. Children with diphtheria or shigellosis could be excluded from school if this was considered necessary to control an outbreak. In the past, people who had or might have smallpox could be placed in quarantine. There are no powers to compel treatment, and the commitment to hospital or quarantine is for short periods.

Links with other Health Purchasing Organisations

One of the weaknesses of public health services in Britain has been the separation of primary, secondary and preventive care. In 1974, the re-organisation of the NHS moved public health into district health authorities from local health authorities, but there was no integration with the family health services until very recently. More separation is occurring in hospital and community services because of competing NHS trusts and independent (private) nursing homes.

An important facet of the link between public health and Family Health Services Authorities (FHSA) is the quality of infection control procedures in general practice. Given the responsibility to protect the public from hepatitis B, HIV and infection in general, the reliability of disinfection and sterilisation is essential. It is probably fair to say that the observance of infection precautions has been more rigorous in general dental practice than in general medical practice. This is partly because dentistry is seen as a surgical discipline, and cases of blood-borne infection have been linked to surgery. As more surgery is done in general medical practice, the public will rightly expect improvements to be made. Most of the monitoring of general practice is done by medical advisers. Most of the day-to-day infection control work in the community, in the surgery, health centre, GP hospital, and nursing home, is done by a combination of disciplines. There is a strong public health interest in ensuring that the training and monitoring in general practice includes some expertise in infection control, and that all staff are fully involved in these activities.

Purchasing Functions

The change for health authorities from management to purchasing health care has not been straightforward partly because the detailed cost of health care has been uncertain. This is especially true of infection which has a number of indirect and opportunity costs that should be accounted for in a proper costing exercise, whilst the benefits of preventing outbreaks is even more intangible. Nevertheless, the clear distinction between those who are managing the health care provided, from those who are defining and measuring what should be provided has sharpened the requirements for infection control in the hospital and community NHS trusts. Usually the public health physician advises the purchasers on the standards and policies that are required for infection control, and can discuss the ways in which these should be assessed. There is a danger of unrealistic expectations, but this has been reduced by the enrolment of microbiologists to be Consultants in Communicable Disease Control and so part of the purchasing organisations. The drawbacks of the separation between purchasing and providing are the time spent by senior people in negotiations on contracts and the extra costs of having to negotiate with many different bodies.

The change has also helped to bring the independent (private) health care sector closer to the NHS. Whilst this raises political issues, it is now easier for public health staff to insist on similar standards of infection control across the range of residential health care services.

In contrast to the sharper focus in the services provided in hospitals and nursing homes and community NHS trusts, the dual role of general practitioners as purchasers (fundholders and representatives on commissioning bodies) and providers is complicated. This is even more complicated when GPs are the medical officers to nursing homes or have other managerial duties. The independent contractors status of general practitioners makes them solely liable for failures to implement infection control procedures. Hopefully, this should make them more conscious of infection control matters. Against this hope must be placed the worry caused by recent guidance from the NHS Executive encouraging GPs to do more surgical treatments themselves, when there is little guidance on sterilisation procedures suitable for general practice premises. There is nothing to compare with the well established guidelines on infection control in hospitals.

What purchasers would like is to be able to rely on clauses in contracts to the effect that 'the providers will comply with health and safety at work legislation' and 'will observe good practice in infection control'. To be reliable, such clauses must be understood by both parties to the contract. In the absence of a clear understanding, it is possible that infection control in the community will be defined in the law courts.

Assessing Health Care Needs

Rational purchasing of health care requires good understanding of what care is needed and worth buying. This is becoming one of the key functions of public health physicians. As new technology and more old people add to the pressure on health budgets, so value for money becomes more important. At present, needs assessment is done by surveillance (to know what infections are present); by keeping up-to-date with new techniques, treatments and vaccines (to know what infections can be prevented); by studying the effectiveness of these new methods; and by public consultation to learn about the priorities and acceptability of present and proposed services. This work should be a combination of local activity, especially to consult with patients and the public, and national or regional research. Too often this combination has been reversed, because the only formal democratic mechanism to make decision on health care is in the British Parliament, while too many innovations have been local developments without proper independent evaluation. This has been as true for public health as it is for clinical practice, and one of the promising features of modern public health is that it is trying to change health care to practice based on public participation and robust assessments.

REFERENCE
1. Department of Health and Social Security. Public Health in England. Report of the Committee of Inquiry into the future development of the Public Health Function. London: HMSO, 1986.

Mr Michael Eastwood

Chapter 11

Infection Control and Environmental Health

Introduction

Environmental health was defined by the World Health Organisation in 1950 as: "The control of all factors in the environment which exercise a harmful effect on human physical development, health and survival."

Environmental health services therefore cover a wide range of activities and whilst throughout the country there may be some minor variations in the nature and level of service delivery there are underlying key aims and objectives of the service. These are:

· the protection of health;
· the prevention of infection;
· the prevention of injury;
· the protection and improvement of the environment;
· the improvement of safety;
· the improvement of living conditions.

Environmental health in England is administered and provided as a local government function and each local district council provides the service to its population. Departments are staffed by qualified environmental health officers and scientific and technical support staff. Areas of work include air pollution control, noise control, food safety, health and safety, housing standards, infectious disease control, port health, and rodent and pest control. Those activities that are specific to infection control within the community are food and water controls, infectious disease control, hazardous waste disposal, rodent and pest control, some aspects of housing standards, licensing and port health.

Many aspects of the work of an environmental health officer have an impact upon preventing the spread of infection within the community. For example departments are often involved in collection services for discarded needles and syringes, or assisting, through health education campaigns, in informing the public about such things as the safe storage of foods.

In a short chapter it is not possible to cover all aspects of the work which have a relevance to infection control, so a sample of the most relevant is presented to give the reader an insight into the contribution made by the environmental health service.

Most, but not all, of the work undertaken by environmental health officers is covered by statute and no attempt has been made, other than as a passing reference, to describe the specifics of the laws and regulations. The legal powers available are significant, particularly with regard to the right of entry to premises and the prosecution of offenders. Whilst it is essential to have legislative controls to protect the public health the law is only used after careful consideration of all of the facts, or if there is an imminent risk of danger to health. In practice a mixture of routine inspection and surveillance with recourse to enforcement is used along with the targeting of resources to deal with specific issues or needs.

Service Delivery

The provision of an environmental health service can be traced back to the middle of the nineteenth century, the start of the public health service and the earliest days of local government as we know it today. Environmental health services have always been delivered at the point of need, be that at an individual's home, place of work, leisure facility, or in the case of foodstuffs at the point of manufacture, preparation, or sale.

The environmental health service does not operate in isolation and in many situations the environmental health officer (EHO) is working in partnership with others or in support of others. The other agencies and officers that interface with EHOs in infection control are the Public Health Laboratory Service, the veterinary service of the Ministry of Agriculture Fisheries and Food, and the Consultant in Communicable Disease Control of the local District Health Authority.

Infection Control

There is a range of functions which are carried out by environmental health officers which are designed directly or indirectly to prevent the incidence or spread of infection. Sources of infection in the community which are of concern include food and water-borne organisms, insect and rodent vectors and transmission via the use of contaminated equipment used for such things as tattooing. The following aspects have been selected to provide an insight into the role and responsibilities of an environmental health officer in the area of infection control.

Food Safety

Infection caused by the consumption of unfit or contaminated foodstuffs has been a cause of concern since humankind became established as a community dweller. Moses, in the Old Testament, said, "Thou shalt not eat the flesh of an animal that dieth of itself, but thou may feed it to a stranger residing in your house." This surely was not meant to be the first example of fraudulent food practice! Perhaps it would have been better presented in a different way!

In England there has been, since the recording of food poisoning cases began in (1948), a steady but alarming increase in the numbers of recorded cases. There is a number of reasons for this increase; some simple such as the increasing awareness of the public, some more complex such as the development of new methods for the preparation and storage of food. Although it is the larger outbreaks of food poisoning which receive publicity and sometimes give cause for concern it is the single incidents which account for the majority of the annual total.

The Environmental Health Department has a range of duties and responsibilities with regard to food safety and food control. The programme of work includes:

- the inspection and sampling of food at wholesale markets, at food processing plants, at warehouses and retail points of sale, as well as at the wide variety of catering establishments that now exist;
- the inspection and surveillance of food handling practices including the identification of hazardous situations;
- the training of personnel in food hygiene;
- the production and dissemination of information to the public on food safety issues.

Food safety surveillance involves an understanding of the three "P's". That is **PEOPLE, PRACTICES, PREMISES**.

PEOPLE. All food processing or preparation involves human control or the handling of food and it is essential that people know and understand the basics of food hygiene and appreciate how they can prevent food from becoming contaminated with micro-organisms, or how to prevent organisms from multiplying to harmful numbers.

PRACTICES. The manner in which foodstuffs are processed, prepared and stored has an obvious effect upon the hygienic quality of the food. Such aspects as temperature control, or the separation of cooked and uncooked foods, are important determinants in preventing contamination or limiting the growth of food poisoning organisms.

PREMISES. The nature of a building, its layout, the ventilation system, the level of illumination are all important in preventing the contamination of food. A building which is cramped does little to encourage good practices, and a building which has inappropriate surfaces which may be difficult to clean can provide harbourage for bacteria and encourage insect activity.

Food is a potential source of infection in that, given the right conditions of moisture, warmth and time, even a small number of food poisoning organisms can quickly multiply to sufficient numbers to cause illness. Food after all is not just a source of nutrition to humans, it also serves that purpose to a wide spectrum of living things, some microscopic, some with little legs, some with wings, the latter two may of themselves add more of the microscopic variety.

The main piece of legislation designed to control food is the Food Safety Act 1990, the principal requirements of the act are:
- the registration of all food premises. This involves notifying the local authority of the address and nature of the business;
- the requirement to visit all food premises at frequencies dependant on risk;
- powers to serve improvement or prohibition notices on the owners of businesses where there is a risk of food causing illness.

Notification of Infectious Diseases

Notifiable diseases which are defined in the Public Health (Control of Disease) Act 1984 have to be formally notified to the 'proper officer' of the local authority by the doctor who makes the diagnosis. The 'proper officer' is usually the Consultant in Communicable Disease Control (CCDC) of the local District Health Authority who is appointed to the local authority to deal with and advise on a number of issues. The environmental health officer plays a part in the surveillance and investigation of notifications of infectious diseases and will be particularly concerned with food related illness.

Water

Drinking Water

The potential for drinking water to contribute to the spread of disease is large if hygiene standards are not maintained. Outbreaks of the more traditional diseases, e.g. cholera, associated with drinking water are not encountered in the UK today, because water collection, distribution and purification systems in the UK are extensive and designed to ensure that each household receives a supply of safe drinking water.

There is, however, a need to remain informed about the quality of drinking water and abreast of changes that may impact upon the supply. In order to address this it is usual for arrangements to be in place whereby the Environmental Health Officers and the Consultants in Communicable Disease Control meet with a range of staff from the regional water company at set intervals so that information can be shared and, if necessary, concerns expressed.

Over the past decade concern has arisen over the possible introduction and distribution of the protozoon Cryptosporidium through the water supply system. Any outbreaks associated with the mains water supply would be 'explosive' and, in order to be prepared, both the local authority and the health authority have to have in place a plan to deal with any outbreak. The EHO would have contributed to the response plan and if an outbreak occurred would be a member of the team assembled to deal with the public health aspects.

There is still a relatively large number of properties which are not connected to the mains water supply and which rely upon a 'private' supply from wells or surface collection systems. These are usually properties in more rural locations which are remote from the mains supply. The quality of these supplies is variable and the environmental health officer will from time to time take samples to determine if there is bacteriological or chemical contamination.

Leisure Water

The quality of water in swimming pools is subject to regular testing by pool operators, and the environmental health officer as part of a routine surveillance programme will visit to check records and if necessary take water samples for testing. The risks of a swimmer contracting illness from a visit to a swimming pool are very low because modern controls over water disinfection are very effective. Visits by EHOs are useful checks on the efficiency of the treatment and the hygiene standards applied by management.

There has been a major increase in the leisure use of water with windsurfing, dinghy sailing, water skiing, scuba diving and fishing being popular recreational activities undertaken by a growing number of people. From time to time concerns arise because of the risks of illness from ingesting water containing the toxins produced by the blue-green algae. Blue-green algae are present in marine, estuarine and fresh water pools, lakes and reservoirs. Usually they are present in low numbers and are of no consequence to public health. At certain times when conditions are favourable the algae can bloom rapidly and produce toxins. Ingestion of water containing the toxin has been found to be toxic to dogs and farm stock. Humans are also therefore considered to be at risk of illness and death. The National Rivers Authority will notify the local authority concerned if the toxin is found in any water above a defined alert level. The environmental health department then has the responsibility of deciding on the best course of action. This is usually decided after discussion with the Consultant in Communicable Disease Control and actions may include the closure of, say, a water park or the introduction of limitations on the type of leisure activity that may take place. The production of algae blooms is seasonal and is influenced by the water temperature and the amount of nutrient present in the water, therefore problems are most likely to occur in the summer or early autumn which coincides with the period of greatest leisure use.

Legionnaires' Disease
The organism which causes Legionnaires' Disease, *Legionella pneumophila*, is widespread in natural and man-made water systems. The organism can therefore be found in water used in air-conditioning systems, cooling towers, and in long runs of plumbing used in such buildings as hotels and office blocks where the water may stand for long periods in a warm environment. *Legionella* grows readily at temperatures between 20°C and 40°C and if the water becomes airborne as an aerosol of particle size less than approximately 5 microns in diameter it may be inhaled and lead to infection. The steps to limit the risks are designed to control the growth of the organism in water systems, and to minimise the production of fine water aerosols. Temperature controls, scheduled specified cleaning of systems and equipment, the fitting of drift eliminators to cooling towers, the installation of self-draining shower heads and the elimination of 'dead legs' in plumbing systems are examples of methods of control.

The EHO, when visiting office and hotel premises, will check on the cleaning and control system that are in place and will offer comment and advice on the adequacy of systems.

Licensing and Registration

Local authorities are assigned a range of licensing and registration functions which are applied to a variety of activities, premises and persons. The purpose of the licence or the registration is to ensure that the health, safety and welfare of the public are protected, whether they are attending a pop concert or riding in a taxi.

Many of the licensing and registration requirements are designed to protect the public health, and the environmental health department deals with such things as the registration of dairies and distributors of milk, to the licensing of camping and caravan sites. The following section considers an area where registration is used to limit the risk of disease transmission through the potential use of 'dirty' equipment.

Acupuncture, Tattooing, Ear Piercing and Electrolysis

Any activity which involves the piercing of skin carries an obvious risk of transmission of infection if hygiene controls or sterilisation techniques are not maintained. The increase in the numbers of premises offering these practices or services led to controls being introduced, with the powers being made available to the local authority. The Local Government (Miscellaneous Provisions) Act 1982 allowed each local authority the option of bringing the relevant controls into force in their area.

Once in force, any person who carries on the practice of acupuncture, or the business of tattooing, ear piercing or electrolysis must register with the local authority (LA). The LA, in addition to registering the person who will be operating the business, will also register the premises. In this way, it is possible to be aware of the location of each activity within a district. The LA may make byelaws in order to ensure that risks of infection being transmitted from client to client are minimised. The byelaws should address:

a) the cleanliness of the registered premises and the fittings on those premises;

b) the cleanliness of the registered person and any person who assists;

c) the cleaning and, if appropriate, the sterilisation of instruments, materials and equipment.

The environmental health department of the local authority will be responsible for the registration and inspection of the business. Any person who fails to operate within the byelaws may be prosecuted by the local authority and if convicted may, as well as or in place of a fine, have their registration suspended or cancelled. Any suspension or cancellation relates to the premises as well as to the registered person. The way in which controls to protect the public health can be designed and applied is well illustrated in this example. It is also another example of the three Ps approach with attention being directed towards the person, the premises and the practices.

Pest and Rodent Control

As well as causing damage to goods, foodstuffs and property, pests and rodents can play a part in the transmission of some diseases. Taking food as an example of the damage and losses caused by insect pests and rodents, it has been estimated that throughout the world many millions of tonnes are lost or spoiled each year.

Public health concern is obviously focused upon the disease transmission potential of both insects and rodents; the presence of either is often indicative of low hygiene or inadequate sanitation, which are themselves indicators of poor management practices and procedures within the premises. In the past the part played by insects and rodents in spreading diseases was of significant concern. For example, the part played by the rat and the flea in the bubonic plague epidemics of the sixteenth and seventeenth centuries in England have been well documented. Whilst today in this country insect pests and rodents are still considered to be of concern, most of the concern relates to the factors that have led to the infestation. If one considers an infestation of say mice or cockroaches within a restaurant kitchen it is accepted that no one wants to find mice droppings in their meal or think that a cockroach has trod through the dessert, but proving that their presence has caused actual illness is difficult. It is therefore more appropriate to deal with infestations as indicators of low hygiene standards, defective sanitation and poor management.

It has been traditional for most local authorities to operate a comprehensive pest and rodent control service but some councils have contracted the treatment aspect to the private sector. In those circumstances the Environmental Health Department retains the control of surveillance and monitoring. In many departments there will be one or two environmental health officers who have gained considerable experience and expertise in the identification of insects and the application of eradication and control techniques for both rodents and insects.

Most local authorities provide a free service for those infestations in domestic premises that are of public health concern, this usually includes treatment for the eradication of fleas, bed bugs, lice, mice, and rats. Treatment for other pests or within commercial premises is provided on a fee paying basis.

Local authorities have a statutory duty to take steps as far as is practicable to ensure that their district is free of rats and mice. This duty is placed on them by the Prevention of Damage by Pests Act 1949, which requires the authority to inspect its area from time to time, to destroy rats or mice on premises that the authority occupies and to ensure that other owners and occupiers take steps to eradicate rats and mice.

In urban areas both older buildings and those of more modern construction can present specific pest control problems. Older commercial buildings may now be in multiple use with a number of quite different businesses being carried out within one building. If an infestation of, say, rodents or cockroaches occurs in one part of the building or in a specific business then it is quite possible that it will spread through the building and add difficulties to the treatment and eradication. Similarly the adjacent buildings in the block may become infested in a relatively short time. In these circumstances the local authority can undertake what is called block treatment. The authority has to give seven days notice to each occupier specifying the nature of the works it is going to undertake. The costs may then be recovered from the occupiers. Block treatments can involve considerable amounts of work but they are the only effective way of dealing with infestations which become established in large multi-use buildings.

In certain system-build housing schemes of the 1960s and 1970s the heating was provided from a central boiler house which served a number of blocks. Each unit of accommodation was linked to the adjacent units and the central boiler house by means of pipes run within trunking. Once cockroaches were introduced to just one flat they spread not just through whole blocks but through the whole estate or development. Attempting to deal with individual units has little effect and some environmental health departments have developed specific block and multi-block treatment strategies which often require the temporary rehousing of the occupants whilst major treatments take place.

Despite the advancement of healthcare and the improvement both in the general welfare and the environment of the public, the challenges facing Environmental Health Officers today are as difficult as they were at the inception of the service in the nineteenth century. This may be due in part to the improved methods of surveillance and reporting, increasing the infection prevention and control aspects of the role.

The Department of Environmental Health in each Local Authority contributes to the management of major outbreaks of infection not only in the community, but also those arising in hospitals and the EHO is normally an active member of the Infection Control Committees.

FURTHER READING

Clay's Environmental Health Officers Handbook
Edited by Davies & Bassett, London: Chapman & Hall, 1992.

Benenson A S, et al. Control of Communicable Disease in Man. 15th ed. Washington, DC. American Public Health Association, 1990.

The Essential Guide to Food Hygiene
by Graham Aston and John Tiffney. Walton-on Thames. Eaton Publications, 1994.

Mrs Jennifer East

Chapter 12

Guidance to Risk Management

The concept of risk addresses the probability that an untoward incident will occur. An untoward incident results from a set of circumstances which may cause harmful consequences, the likelihood of it happening is the risk associated with it. The degree of risk and the possible consequences can be increased or decreased by the impact of various risk factors. Some risk factors, such as toxins and infectious agents, are present in the physical environment; some, such as smoking, lack of effective handwashing and driving without seat-belts, are behavioural; some, such as instability or socio-economic deprivation, are part of the social environment; and some, such as predispositions to certain diseases, are hereditary. Often there is no clear relationship between a risk factor and a specific outcome. For example, devitalised tissue in a surgical wound is known to predispose in infection. However, while some surgeons do not tie off all bleeding vessels or eliminate dead spaces their patients do not inevitably develop infected wounds; conversely some superb surgeons may occasionally have patients who do. In the health care setting professionals have a responsibility to identify risks over which they have some control and to take appropriate measures to minimise those risks.[1] This process when actively undertaken is referred to as risk management.

Risk Management

This is a systematic process of risk identification, analysis, deciding what action is required and evaluation of potential and actual risks. The primary purposes are to safeguard the assets of the organisation by identifying and controlling the risks before financial losses occur; or to continue to function in the event of a major loss without severe hardship to the financial stability of the organisation.[2]

Risk management provides a mechanism for risk reduction, and elimination and avoidance of economic losses. It has to be a planned programme, requiring commitment from management, clinical staff and all employees, to prevent, control and monitor risk factors.

The Origin of Risk Management

Risk management has emerged as an operational component of health care as a result of:
- rising health care costs
- the Government's need to contain costs
- the development of the division between the purchaser and provider of health care
- increasing numbers of claims against providers of health care
- escalating court settlements.

The Goals of Risk Management

There are many reasons for establishing and implementing an effective risk management programme; the objectives are:
- to ensure the survival of the organisation following a major loss, by providing sufficient assets to regain pre-loss status and freedom from worry about a potential loss
- to enhance the quality and standard of care
- to minimise the risk of clinical or accidental injuries and losses
- to ensure the programme's effectiveness and efficiency through management direction and control
- to co-ordinate and integrate current policies, programmes, committees and all aspects of the risk management process
- to avoid adverse publicity as the result of litigation.

The Risk Management Process

To effectively manage identified risks it is necessary to follow a formal cyclical process, which consists of five main steps:
- identification of the problem or risk;
- analysis of the actual/potential risk;
- identification of possible solutions;
- implementation of the agreed corrective action;
- evaluation of the effectiveness of this action and monitoring the effect on the incidence of the risk.

Step 1: Risk Identification
a   Risk identification requires a systematic process of identifying actual and potential losses as distinct from haphazard identification. It is the most important step because unless they are identified, risks are not managed effectively. It is also important as it is the first step in deciding the best corrective action to implement.

b. A prerequisite for risk identification is a thorough understanding of:
- the nature and scope of the services provided in a particular environment, whether diagnostic or therapeutic, and of the equipment and supplies used;
- the legislation and regulations affecting the provision of care;
- the potential liability incurred as a result of providing those services, assessed on the basis of the previous claims history and information gathered, e.g. from incident/accident reporting and local audits.

When carrying out this process it is likely that a number of risks will be identified and the volume of information gathered may become overwhelming. It is necessary therefore to prioritise the risks which are identified to ensure that the risk management process becomes more effective. This process should identify:
- the probable or possible severity of the loss;
- the likelihood of the risk;
- any trends or patterns;
- how much it will cost to eliminate or reduce the risk;
- whether the problem requires immediate action.

Step 2: Analysis of Actual or Potential Risks
The risk or local manager must determine which exposures require action and which can be safely ignored. There are several ways to approach this:
- to determine the likely severity of the risk exposure by using past claims experience, incident/accident report data, local or external experience
- to determine the effect of the potential loss on the organisation; that is whether there would be adverse publicity on a loss of contract and subsequent revenue
- to integrate subjective opinions and objective data obtained from legal council, insurance company input, risk management, health and safety groups.

Step 3: Identification of Possible Risk Solutions
When deciding which solution would be the most appropriate there are three stages which should be considered:
- not performing a procedure rather than accepting the risk associated with it;
- introducing suitable controls;
- implementing relevant controls to reduce the potential severity of the risk.

The key to selecting the best course of action is to identify the technique that contributes to the most cost effective approach of managing the risk.

Step 4: Implementing the Agreed Risk Solution
- the solution should be agreed by those who are affected by the risk or those who have a responsibility to ensure the safety of others, whether they are patients, staff, contractors or visitors;
- it may be necessary to introduce new techniques, equipment or working practices;
- where major changes are made to working practices it will be necessary to devise and agree new policies and protocols;
- where there is a change in practice, technique or equipment then suitable training programmes for staff will be required.

Step 5: Evaluation and Monitoring
This step requires a continuous assessment of the effectiveness of the risk management process:
> this is evaluated by a decrease in the incidence of the previously identified problem, such as:
> - a reduction in the number of incidents/accidents;
> - a reduction in the number of claims;
> - fewer patient complaints;
> - fewer injuries;
> - a decrease in the number of adverse patient outcomes.

Practical Aspects of the Process

In the community there are specific risks to be addressed:
1. There must be a safety policy,[3] modified to take local features into account. This policy must identify the risks and safe practices associated with:
   - the specific working environment;
   - the assessment of factors relevant to the Control of Substances Hazardous to Health (COSHH) assessments;[4]
   - the assessment of manual handling operations;[5]
   - the assessment of visual display unit (VDU) operations;[6]
   - infection control protocols.
2. Essential elements for an effective risk assessment programme:
   - these include training of all staff particularly managers and safety representatives to enable them to recognise what needs to be assessed and what controls are needed to minimise any risks;
   - it will also be necessary to establish safe systems of work and to ensure that these are complied with.
3. An appropriate audit tool should be devised; there are many examples available which can be reviewed and adapted to local needs. An area of safety assessment which is frequently not reviewed is the patient's home, often because it is seen as being difficult to control (Appendix I).
4. Elements in the environment which need to be assessed include:
   - heating, lighting, ventilation;
   - hygiene and cleanliness;
   - waste storage and disposal;[7]
   - fire and electrical safety;
   - noise, dust;
   - toxic materials, handling and disposal;
   - first aid provision;
   - staff protection and welfare.

To ensure that the patients' infection risks are identified they should be assessed as part of the care planning process and regularly re-evaluated. It can be helpful to consider the potential risks by reviewing the patients using a simple assessment tool which can be reassessed on a regular basis using the same criteria (See Appendix II).

In conclusion it is the responsibility of everybody in health care to ensure that they are knowledgeable about all risk aspects of their work, what their personal risks are and the appropriate protective measures necessary to maintain their own, their colleagues and their patients' safety.

REFERENCES
1. Jackson M M, Lynch P. Applying an epidemiological structure to risk management and quality assurance activities. Quality Review Bulletin 1985; 306-12.
2. Department of Health. Risk management in the NHS Department of Health. London: DOH, 1993.
3. Department of Health. Health and Safety at Work Act, etc. London: HMSO, 1974.
4. Department of Health. Health and Safety Control of substances hazardous to health regulations. London: HMSO, 1988.
5. Department of Health. Health and Safety Manual handling operations regulations. London: HMSO, 1992.
6. Health and Safety Display screen equipment regulations. London: HMSO, 1992.
7. Department of Environment Waste management - the duty of care. A code of practice. London: HMSO, 1991.

Appendix I

RISK ASSESSMENT (PATIENTS HOME)
Note: Risks to both the patient and care staff should be identified.

Name: .... Age: ....

Address: ....

....

....

.... Postcode ....

Primary diagnosis: ....

Reason for Visit: ....

RISK ASSESSMENT (please tick the appropriate box)

General Environmental Risks:	High:	Medium:	Low/No risk
Car parking safety	☐	☐	☐
Location of home	☐	☐	☐
House	☐	☐	☐
Flat in house	☐	☐	☐
Flat in block	☐	☐	☐
Other	☐	☐	☐

General household risks:			
Entrance to home	☐	☐	☐
Carpets, flooring, etc.	☐	☐	☐
Furniture	☐	☐	☐
Bed, bedding	☐	☐	☐
Work area/ clutter, trailing wires etc	☐	☐	☐
Animals	☐	☐	☐
Washing facilities	☐	☐	☐
Waste disposal	☐	☐	☐
Other	☐	☐	☐

Patient Care Risks:			
Mobility	☐	☐	☐
Manual handling needs	☐	☐	☐
Communication	☐	☐	☐
Hygiene needs	☐	☐	☐
Wound / tissue viability	☐	☐	☐
Invasive procedures: injections/ infusions/catheters, etc.	☐	☐	☐

NOTE: Where risks are identified as high explain reasons for assessment and then develop and record risk reduction strategies in the patient's record.